NO-
SWEAT
SCIENCE

Nature
Experiments

ANTHONY D. FREDERICKS

Illustrated by Dave Garbot

STERLING PUBLISHING CO., INC.
NEW YORK

AUG 2006

**Library of Congress Cataloging-in-Publication Data
Available**

10 9 8 7 6 5 4 3 2 1

Published by Sterling Publishing Co., Inc.
387 Park Avenue South, New York, NY 10016
© 2005 by Sterling Publishing Co., Inc.
Previously published as *Simple Nature Experiments with Everyday Materials,*
© 1995 by Anthony D. Fredericks
Illustrations © 2005 by Dave Garbot
Distributed in Canada by Sterling Publishing
c/o Canadian Manda Group, 165 Dufferin Street
Toronto, Ontario, Canada M6K 3H6
Distributed in Great Britain and Europe by Chris Lloyd at Orca Book
Services, Stanley House, Fleets Lane, Poole BH15 3AJ, England
Distributed in Australia by Capricorn Link (Australia) Pty. Ltd.
P.O. Box 704, Windsor, NSW 2756, Australia

Sterling ISBN 1-4027-2158-7

For information about custom editions, special sales, premium and
corporate purchases, please contact Sterling Special Sales
Department at 800-805-5489 or specialsales@sterlingpub.com.

To Michael, Ben, and Brian Roll.
May their world be ever green!

CONTENTS

BEFORE YOU BEGIN

You may not realize it, but you are related to the dragonfly. You are also related to the pine tree and the mushroom. In fact, all living organisms are related to each other in some way. We depend on members of the plant and animal kingdoms for our food, for building and clothing materials, and for our enjoyment. Plants and animals depend on each other for their survival, too. In fact, all plants and animals (including human beings like you and me) are part of a complex survival system, commonly called the **ecology**, with every other member of the plant and animal worlds.

The activities in this book are designed to help you explore and understand nature and to appreciate the connections that exist between all living things and the world around them. You will discover that you alone can do a lot to help the environment where you live. You may also be able to work together with others to help preserve your environment. That is the way we learn to really appreciate the plants and animals with whom we share this world, and also how we can ensure that we will be able to enjoy them for years to come.

This is a book of discovery. All of the activities are hands-on, are fun to do, and use only simple, easy-to-obtain materials. Some activities will take only a few minutes; others will last several days or weeks. Most of the activities are open-ended, meaning there are no right or wrong answers. You can do as many of the experiments as you wish, again and again, or for as long as you want. You are the scientist.

Several of the activities suggest that you keep a journal or notebook to record your observations. Scientists always do this. Buy a spiral notebook and mark it "My Nature Journal." Use your journal to keep track of the growth of a plant, the animals you see in a certain area, or how much rain fell on a certain day. Your journal will be an important record of what you did and observed during an experiment so that you can compare it to what happens when you do the same experiment again several weeks or months later.

If an activity doesn't seem to be working correctly, don't get discouraged. Try it again, maybe at another time or in a different location. Feel free to modify parts of an activity to better suit the conditions where you live. Look into your own special questions or interests and follow wherever they lead. Scientists do this all the time. They start out with one question and, during the course of an experiment, come up with a dozen new questions to look into. You will probably do the same thing, and all your new questions, observations, and discoveries can be recorded in your nature journal.

An inexpensive camera can be a big help in your nature study. Putting photographs of a bean plant, taken over several weeks, in your journal is a wonderful reminder of what you observed and learned. Taking pictures of all kinds of animal life can also yield some astonishing photos.

The activities in this book can be done in any order and whenever you want. They have been designed to help you learn about and appreciate nature. They are also designed to be fun and to provide you with hours of fascinating discoveries. I hope you enjoy them!

Be Smart/Be Safe

It's smart to be careful in whatever you do. A few of these experiments or activities call for the use of a stove, a knife, or a sharp scissors—times when you might want to ask an adult for help. Watch for the "safety bee" in the following pages to remind you, and *do* be careful.

UNDERGROUND

When you walk through a park, over a hill, or down a dusty road, you probably don't give much thought to the ground under your feet. But the ground is an important part of nature. The soil we use to grow our plants and the rocks we use to build our homes and highways are valuable in many ways.

Soil is mostly made up of rock that has been broken up into very small pieces. This sand, created over hundreds of thousands of years, is the result of weather, erosion, and freezing and thawing. Soil also contains air, water, and decayed matter (known as **humus**). Basically, there are three types of soil: clay, sand, and **loam** (a rich mixture of clay, sand, and humus that is good for growing plants).

There are also three different kinds of rocks. **Igneous** rock, such as granite, is formed from melted minerals, so it is often found near volcanoes. **Sedimentary** rock usually forms underwater, as a result of layers of material, called sediment, pressing down on other layers. Sandstone and limestone are examples of this type of rock. **Metamorphic** rock, such as marble, is formed by the great heat and pressure deep inside the Earth's surface.

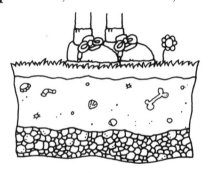

The experiments here will help you learn about the soil and rock in your special part of the world.

Rock and Roll

The sand in soil is rock that has been broken up and worn down by a process called erosion. To demonstrate this, you need to make your own rocks (most outdoor rocks are much too hard).

You need:

clean sand

a small container

aluminum foil

a coffee can (with lid)

white glue

a plastic spoon

water

WHAT TO DO:

Mix three large spoonfuls of sand together with three spoonfuls of white glue. Make small lumps of the mixture and place them on a lightly oiled piece of aluminum foil, so that they will not stick to it. Put the "rocks" in a dry, sunny location for two or three days, until hard. Then put some of your "rocks" into the coffee can with some water. Hold the lid on securely and shake the can for four to five minutes. Remove the lid.

WHAT HAPPENS:

The rocks begin to wear down. Some rocks may be worn down into sand again.

WHY:

The water running over the rocks pushes them against each other, causing erosion that wears them down. In nature, this process takes many years, but the result is the same. Rocks are broken up, become smaller from rubbing against each other, and over time wear down into sandy particles that may eventually become part of the soil near a river or stream.

It's a Dirty Job . . .

The surface of our Earth is made up of rocks, sand, humus, water, and air. All of these soil "ingredients" are necessary for plants and animals to survive. Let's find out how much air is in different soils.

You need:
small clear jars
water
soil samples

WHAT TO DO:
Half fill each jar with a soil sample from several places in your neighborhood. Fill the rest of the jars with water, almost to the top.

WHAT HAPPENS:
Depending on the soil you are testing, you will see a few, some, or a lot of air bubbles rising to the top of the water in each jar. The number of bubbles tell how much air was trapped in the spaces between the soil particles.

WHY:
The more bubbles rising through the water, the more air was trapped in the soil sample. Tightly packed soil has less space for air to be trapped than does soil that has a lot of humus or other organic matter in it to make air pockets. Most plants tend to grow better in such aerated soil (soil with lots of air pockets) than densely packed soil (such as clay).

Soak It Up

Good soil, like that in a garden, always has some water in it. Here's how to find it.

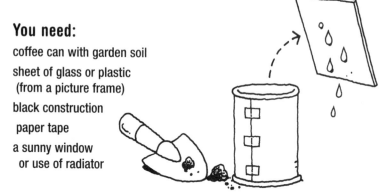

You need:

coffee can with garden soil

sheet of glass or plastic
(from a picture frame)

black construction
paper tape

a sunny window
or use of radiator

WHAT TO DO:

Fill the can about half full of garden soil. Tape a piece of black construction paper around the can and place the glass or plastic over the top. Put the can in a sunny window or on a warm radiator for a couple of hours.

WHAT HAPPENS:

Water droplets begin to form on the underside of the lid. To prove that the water is from the soil, not the air, clean out and dry the can and repeat the experiment, but without putting in any soil. Compare the results.

WHY:

All soil contains some water. How much is held by the soil depends on what else is in the soil, the outside temperature, the weather at the time, and the climate in the area—wet or dry. Soil water is necessary for plant and animal growth, but most plants will need more water (from rain, rivers, or lakes) to keep growing.

Nutrients Away

The food, or **nutrients**, in the soil can wash away when there is a lot of rain. Here's how it happens.

You need:

$1/_2$ cup (120 mL) dry soil

$1/_4$ teaspoon (1 mL) blue powdered tempera paint (from the hobby or art store)

a measuring spoon

a measuring cup

a wide-mouthed jar

a funnel

a coffee filter

cups or containers

water

WHAT TO DO:

Add the blue tempera paint to the soil and mix thoroughly. Set the funnel in the mouth of the jar and put a coffee filter in the funnel. Pour the soil mixture into the filter. Pour $1/_2$ cup (120 mL) of water into the funnel over the jar. Pour the water in the jar into a cup or container and put the funnel over the jar again; repeat this again with another $1/_2$ cup (120 mL) of water. Pour off the water, and repeat it another two or three times.

WHAT HAPPENS:

At first, the water that flows into the jar will be dark blue in color. Each time more water is poured over the same soil mixture, the color will get lighter. Eventually the water will have no more blue in it and run clear into the jar. How many times did it take for that to happen?

WHY:

The blue tempera paint you added to the soil represents the nutrients that are naturally in the ground. These nutrients are necessary for plants to grow. However, when there is a lot of rain or water runoff, these nutrients are washed away, leaving a nutrient-poor soil. Excessive rains and water runoff can remove from the soil the valuable food and minerals needed for plant growth. If you look at places in your area where a lot of soil has eroded away, you will see that there are very few plants growing there. Any plants still there are the kind that don't need much food to grow.

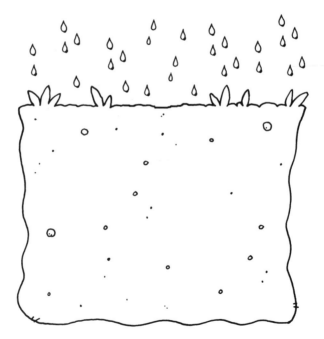

Deeper and Deeper

Soil is made up of different layers. Here's a way you can look for them.

You need:

a small shovel or trowel

tape measure or ruler

small sealable plastic bags

magnifying glass

pencil and paper

sheets of white paper

WHAT TO DO:

Find a place where you can dig a hole (be sure to ask permission first). Try to dig about 2 feet (60 cm) or so straight down. Notice the colors of the soil layers along the sides of the hole as you dig. Measure the distance from the surface down to the different soil layers and write it down. Place a small sample of each layer's soil in a plastic bag.

At home, put some of each sample on clean white paper. Use a magnifying glass or a microscope to examine the samples.

WHAT HAPPENS:

Depending on where you live and dig, you may find one or more soil colors in layers as you dig down.

WHY:

The soil near the surface is usually a dark, rich color. This layer, called **topsoil**, is the thinnest, and it usually contains lots of organic matter (dead and decaying plants, insects, and animals, which make up humus). Topsoil is best for growing plants and food crops. The next layer, known as subsoil, is often lighter in color and has a lot of sand and rocks in it. The last layer of soil is called the bedrock. If you dig down far enough to reach it, you will find that it is the hardest layer to dig through. This is because there is no organic matter to soften it; bedrock is mostly made up of rocks, pebbles, and stones packed tightly together. (Note: Always remember to fill in any holes you make after you have finished obtaining soil samples.)

Making Bricks

You can make your own bricks using the same technique that the early pioneers did.

You need:
ground clay, or a mix of organic
  (not modeling) clay and soil
straw
water
a bucket

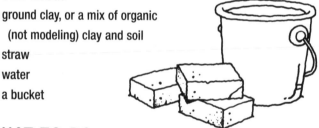

WHAT TO DO:
Put some ground clay (or your own homemade clay), straw, and enough water to make a doughy mixture in a bucket. Mix it together thoroughly. Place portions of the mixture into molds (frozen-vegetable boxes or small waxed cardboard juice containers are good). Let them sit overnight in a warm place, then gently tear away the sides of the molds and let the bricks dry in the sun for several days. Use them to build something, like a little tower or house.

A Crystal Garden

Many of the rocks you find in the Earth's soil were formed by a process known as crystallization. This process goes on all the time and can easily be re-created in your own home. Here's how.

Wet a small piece of brick with water and place it in a small bowl. In a separate large container, mix together $1/_2$ cup (120 mL) water, $1/_2$ cup (120 mL) bluing (from the laundry section of the grocery store), and $1/_2$ cup (120 mL) ammonia (also from the grocery store). Use a measuring cup to pour some of this mixture over the brick. Sprinkle the brick with salt and let it sit for twenty-four hours. The next day you will see crystals forming on the surface of the brick.

Add some more of the water/bluing/ammonia mixture to keep the blue crystals growing. Or you can use drops of other food coloring and change some of the crystals from blue into a colorful display.

From Dust to Dust

When soil is blown from one place to another by the wind, it is known as wind erosion. This is a serious problem in many parts of the world. Is it happening where you live?

You need:

stirring paddles (from the paint store) or wide pointed sticks

double-sided tape

felt marker

WHAT TO DO:

Stick some two-sided tape on one side of several different paddles. Stick the paddle handles into the ground in various places near your home. The paddles should face in different directions—north, south, east, and west (mark the direction on the paddles). At regular intervals—once or twice every week, for example—look at the paddles and record the amount of dust, dirt, or soil sticking to the tape.

WHAT HAPPENS:

Depending on the amount of wind and the direction it blows where you live, you will see that certain paddles collect more dust and dirt than other paddles do.

WHY:

More soil sticks on the paddles where wind erosion is taking place. If there are no barriers, such as trees, plants, and grass, to slow down or stop wind erosion, great quantities of soil can be swept into the air from one location and left somewhere else. One way to prevent wind erosion is to grow trees and plants to cut the wind and to cover and protect the ground. This is why wind erosion is much less of a problem in dense forests than it is in the desert, which has sandstorms!

Erosion Explosion

Erosion can move large quantities of soil and seriously affect the lives of plants and people. Some examples of wind or water erosion are a sandbar in a stream or off a beach, whirling dust devils, a muddy river after a storm, and sand drifted against a fence or in a gully or canyon.

One type of erosion, quite common in and around the home, is called wear. It's caused by friction rather than wind or water. Here are some examples of wear erosion to look for:

1. Coins that are smooth from handling
2. Shoes with the heels worn down
3. An old car tire with no tread
4. A countertop with its design or finish worn away

Can you list more evidence of erosion in and around your home?

Stem the Tide

Plants are important in many ways, but can they do anything to prevent or slow down soil erosion?

You need:

2 cake pans
soil
grass seed
water
a pitcher
2 books

WHAT TO DO:

Fill the cake pans with soil. In one pan, plant some grass seed. Water the soil in both pans equally. Place the pan with the grass seed in a sunny location and water gently for several days. When the grass is about 3 inches (7.5 cm) high, place one end of each pan against a book or block of wood so that they lie at an angle. Fill the pitcher with water and pour the water at the top of the first pan. Do the same thing with the pan that has grass growing in it.

WHAT HAPPENS:

In the pan without grass, the water flows freely across the surface. Some of the dirt is carried by the fast-running water toward the bottom of the pan. In the other pan, with the grass, less soil is washed away.

WHY:

The grass slows down the flow of the water over the surface, and that stops much of the soil from being eroded away. You have looked at mountains or bare hillsides with very few plants and noticed that lots of soil has been washed away, except for rocks too big for the water to move. The use of plants helps keep soil in place and prevents erosion damage.

DID YOU KNOW?

- In the United States alone, more than 7 billion tons (6.3 billion metric tons) of topsoil is eroded away into streams and rivers every year. Because of sedimentation from the Mississippi River in Louisiana and lava accumulation in Hawaii, these states are the only ones that continue to grow in physical size.

- About 75 percent of all rocks on the Earth's surface are sedimentary rocks (rocks formed when small grains and particles of sediment are pressed together under tons of water for long periods of time).

- Each year, the world's deserts grow by as much as 16,000 square miles (41,600 sq km).

WATER, WATER EVERYWHERE

Water is one of the things we often take for granted. We turn on a faucet and water comes out. We turn the faucet off and the water stops. We usually don't think about what water is and just what it means to us, but we should. It is needed for our health, it is an important source of power for business and industry, and it is vital for maintaining life on Earth in all its forms.

One of the major concerns we have about water today is its purity (its cleanliness). Pollution of our water sources and resources is an increasing problem all over the world. We all need to work together to ensure that the water we want to use tomorrow is protected today.

The fun activities in this chapter will help you to learn more about water and its role in nature.

Compact and Loose

Both water and soil are needed for plant growth. But water travels through soil at different rates, depending on how much organic matter there is among the inorganic matter in the soil.

You need:

a measuring cup

potting soil

clean sandbox sand

3 same-size cans (with ends removed)

cheesecloth

scissors

masking tape

water

3 clear jars

a helper,
 or a clock with
 a second hand

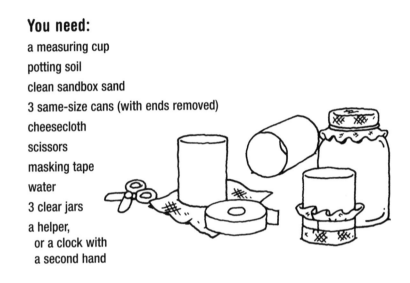

WHAT TO DO:

Cut three squares of cheesecloth big enough to cover the end of the cans. Drape a piece over one end of each can and tape the it around the edges of the can. Cut out three more pieces of cheesecloth and lay them over the tops of the glass jars. Turn the cans over, so the cheesecloth is on the bottom, and half-fill the first can with potting soil. Fill the second can halfway with sand. For the third can, combine potting soil and sand and half-fill the can with the mixture. Use your hand to pack down the soils in each can firmly, then place each can of soil on top of a cheesecloth-covered jar.

If you have a helper with you, add $^1/_2$ cup (120 mL) of water to each can at the same time and see which one the water drips through first. If you are experimenting alone, pour the water into the cans one at a time, watch the jar and clock, and mark the time it takes for the water to leak through the soil packed into each jar.

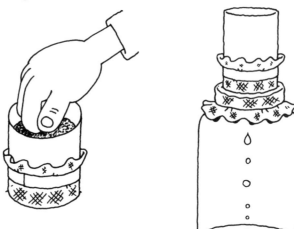

WHAT HAPPENS:

The water you put in the can of sand runs through to the jar much more rapidly than the water in the sand and soil mixture. The water in the mixture leaks through at a faster rate than the water in the potting soil.

WHY:

Water flows through sand very quickly because this soil has lots of air space between the grains that lets the water pass through. Because the potting soil has organic material in it, this soil holds on to more of the water, stopping it from leaking through. This is one reason why gardeners and farmers add humus or other organic matter to the soil–to hold the water for their crops.

The ability of a soil to allow water to pass through it is called **permeability.**

Well, Well, Well

To get a drink of water, you probably just turn on a faucet. Many people, however, get their water from wells. How does this kind of system work? Let's build a small one and see.

You need:
a cardboard tube from
 a roll of toilet paper

a large (coffee) can

aquarium or potting gravel

sand

water

WHAT TO DO:

Place the tube upright in the middle of the coffee can. Holding the tube, pour a layer of about $1^1/_2$ inches (4 cm) of gravel on the bottom of the coffee can around the outside of the tube. Pour a second layer, this time of sand, on top of the gravel. Slowly pour some water onto the sand until the water reaches the top of the sand. Notice what happens inside the tube.

WHAT HAPPENS:

After a short time, water begins to rise inside the tube.

WHY:

When it rains, groundwater collects under the surface of the Earth. Some people think of this groundwater as a series of large underground lakes extending for miles and miles. Because there is a limit to the amount of water that can collect in an area, water pressure builds up in these "lakes." If a well has been dug nearby, the pressure forces water into it, where it can be reached and used.

More Than You Know

If a stream runs near where you live, try this experiment to find out something about the water that flows there.

You need:
your eyes and nose
a clean container

WHAT TO DO:

Visit a nearby stream. Bend down and look closely at the water as it flows by. Sniff the air. Dip your container into the water and raise some to your nose. Smell it again.

WHAT HAPPENS:

Did you notice any of the following conditions?

• Some streams have a rotten-egg smell. Often they are heavily polluted from a lot of sewage being dumped into the water source.

• If the stream has a shiny or multicolored film floating on it, that means that oil or gasoline is seeping into the water.

• If the color of the water is very green, there is probably a lot of algae in the water. Too much algae means there isn't enough oxygen in the water for fish and other plant life.

• Foam or suds floating on the water usually means that detergent or other soapy waste is leaking into the water from nearby factories or homes.

• Cloudy or muddy water usually means that the water contains large quantities of dirt, silt, or mud. Unfortunately, this means that the animals and plants that live in the stream aren't getting enough oxygen. It is possible that a lot of soil erosion is taking place somewhere upstream. Can you do something about it?

• Bright colors, such as red or orange, on the surface of the water is an indication that pollutants are being released into the stream by factories and industries.

Clean, clear water that has no smell to it is the best kind of water for aquatic plants and animals, and for us.

WHY:

For too long, people believed that it was okay to let streams and rivers carry away their pollutants and garbage. People put lots of things into their streams without thinking of the long-term effects. We now know that whatever we put into a stream will affect the plants, animals, and people who live downstream. Cleaning up our streams and making sure we don't put anything into a stream that does not occur naturally in that stream are important steps in maintaining these important, life-giving water sources.

From Shore to Shore

Often when we think about water pollution, we think about rivers and streams. But we need to think about our oceans, too, because much of the food we eat, the weather that affects us, the air, and even the moisture in it comes from our oceans. Unfortunately, even our largest oceans are becoming contaminated—oil spills pollute the sea, litter is thrown into the water, and garbage washes up on shores all over the world.

Even though we don't drink ocean water, it is still important to human life. If you have ever gone to a beach to swim or to walk along the shore, you may have seen some of the pollution that is destroying the world's oceans. Here are three things you can do to help:

1. If you go to a beach, take along a garbage bag to pack up your own litter or any you may find there. Put it in an available trash can or take it away with you when you leave.

2. Cut apart the plastic rings that come with six-packs of canned or bottled drinks. These often find their way into the oceans and can choke and kill sea birds and other marine life.

3. Ask your parents to buy soaps and detergents that are biodegradable and don't poison the ocean. Regular soaps contaminate the liquid waste in sewers, which is often pumped into the oceans and can kill large numbers of sea animals and plants. It is important to use biodegradable products even if you don't live anywhere near the ocean.

Ocean Motion

Would you like to create an ocean that you can keep in your own home?

You need:
a clean plastic bottle
salad oil
water
blue food coloring

WHAT TO DO:
Pour salad oil into the bottle until it is one-third full. Fill the rest of the bottle to the brim with water and add a few drops of blue food coloring. Screw the cap on very tight and lay the bottle on its side. Now, tip the bottle back and forth.

WHAT HAPPENS:
The oily water in the bottle begins to roll back and forth, moving just like the waves in the ocean do. You have created a miniature ocean in a bottle.

WHY:
Waves are energy moving through water. The water of the wave itself doesn't move—it's the energy passing from one water molecule to another that forms the waves. Ocean waves are caused by the gravitational pull of the moon on the Earth's surface water, the shape (geological formation) of the ocean floor, and the spinning of the Earth on its axis. You can create similar conditions artificially in a soda bottle and observe wave action that is very much like what occurs throughout the oceans of the world.

Drip, Drip, Drip

With this experiment you'll be able to remove salt from salt water. Let's try it.

You need:
water
table salt
a measuring cup
measuring spoons
a large bowl
a small cup
plastic wrap
a small stone

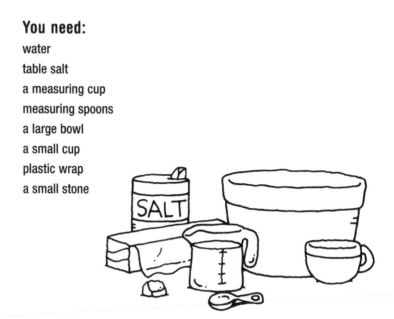

WHAT TO DO:

In the large bowl, mix 1 tablespoon (15 mL) salt into 2 cups (480 mL) of water until it is thoroughly dissolved. Use a spoon to carefully taste a small sample of the salt water. Set the small cup in the middle of the bowl. Cover the bowl with plastic wrap and place a small stone in the center of the wrap (directly over the cup) to weigh the plastic down. Set the wrapped bowl, with stone in place, in the sun for several hours. Look at the wrap after a while and you will notice beads of water forming on the underside of the plastic food wrap and dripping into the small cup. Later on, remove the plastic wrap and taste the water that has collected in the cup.

WHAT HAPPENS:

The salt water inside the large bowl evaporates into the air inside the bowl. It then condenses as beads of water on the underside of the plastic wrap. With the plastic covering lower in the center, the beads of water roll down to the lowest point and drip into the small cup. The water in the cup is no longer salty.

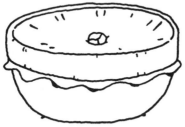

WHY:

This experiment illustrates the natural process of **solar distillation**. Distillation involves changing a liquid into a gas (evaporation) by heating and then back into a liquid (condensation) by cooling the gas vapor. The sun's energy can evaporate water but not salt (salt molecules are heavier than water molecules), so the salt remains in the bowl. The water can now be used for drinking purposes and the salt can be used for food seasoning. This process, often referred to as **desalination** (removing salt), is used in many countries, such as those in the Middle East, to make fresh water from salt water.

You Crack Me Up!

Here's an experiment that demonstrates how large boulders are broken down into tiny pebbles—by water!

You need:
pieces of sandstone
(from the hardware or
building supply store)
sealable plastic bags
water

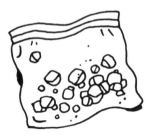

WHAT TO DO:
Soak pieces of sandstone in water overnight. The next day, place several pieces of the wet sandstone into sandwich bags and seal them tightly. Place the bags in the freezer overnight. Take them out and examine them the next day.

WHAT HAPPENS:
The sandstone cracks into smaller pieces.

WHY:
When water freezes, it expands. The sandstone absorbs some of the water, taking it up into the air spaces between the sand particles. When the stone was placed in the freezer, the water in it froze and expanded.

In nature, water seeps into the cracks of rocks, freezes in winter, and causes the rocks to break apart. After a while, the rocks are reduced to very small pebbles and eventually to sand.

Don't Rain on My Parade

Acid rain is a problem in many parts of the world, especially where there is a lot of industry. Here's how to find out if acid rain is a problem where you live.

You need:

small jars

pH paper and color chart (from the aquarium or pet store)

rain and water samples (see below)

tweezers

WHAT TO DO:

Make sure each jar is thoroughly cleaned and dried. With an adult to help, collect several different samples of water (tap water, rainwater, well water, pool water, etc.). Collect each sample in a separate jar. Using the tweezers, dip a strip of pH paper into a sample of water and quickly compare the color that results against the color chart. Do the same for each water sample and record the results. (You may want to collect some rainwater at the beginning of a storm and some at the end of the storm and compare the two different rainwater samples.)

WHAT HAPPENS:

You notice that the various water samples have different pH readings.

WHY:

pH indicates the amount of acid in substances. The pH scale goes from 0 to 14. Pure water, for example, has a pH value of 7 (it is neutral). Substances that have a pH value less than 7 are acids; substances that have a pH value more than 7 are bases. Acids and bases are common chemicals, many of which we have in our homes. Vinegar and lemon juice, for example, are acids, while baking soda is a base. The strength of an acid or base is measured by the pH scale (the lower the number, the more acidic a substance is; the higher a number, the more basic, or alkaline, it is). Acid rain has a pH value of 5.6 or less. Rain that is considerably less than 5.6 on the pH scale will be more damaging to the environment than rain above 5.6 on the pH scale. Rain that falls at the beginning of a storm is usually more acidic than rain that falls at the end of a storm because the acidic compounds in the air are "washed out" of the clouds as the rain continues. Also, the rain that falls in the eastern United States is more acidic (because of the prevailing winds) than rain that falls in the western half of the country.

Type of Water	PH Number
Well	
Rain	
Tap	
Bottled	
Etc...	

Acid Soil

There are many different types of soil. Certain plants (blueberries) like to grow in acid soils, and some plants (potatoes, peaches) prefer basic soils. You can test the pH (acidity or alkalinity) of soil with this experiment.

Collect several soil samples from various places in and around your community (about 1 cup [240 mL] of each will do). In clean jars, mix each soil sample with 1 cup (240 mL) of distilled water. (Distilled water, available in grocery stores, is neutral, having a pH of 7.) Shake each sample thoroughly. After a few minutes, dip a separate strip of pH test paper into each sample and quickly compare the strip to the colors on the pH chart. You should be able to see some difference in the pH of the soils even in your own neighborhood. Invite friends and relatives to give you soil samples from other places for testing, too.

DID YOU KNOW?

- It is estimated that about 14 billion pounds (6.3 billion kg) of trash and garbage are dumped into the oceans of the world every year.

- Americans alone consume about 450 billion gallons (1.7 trillion liters) of water every day.

- Over 99 percent of all the fresh water on Earth is trapped in icebergs, icecaps, and glaciers.

- Mt. Waialeale in Hawaii averages 451 inches (1,146 cm) of rain per year, making it the wettest spot on earth.

- There's about 9 million tons (8.1 million metric tons) of gold dissolved in the oceans of the world.

- From the mouth of the Amazon River in Brazil pours one-fifth of all the moving fresh water on Earth.

- Canada contains one-third of all the fresh water on Earth.

- North America has more than 190,000 miles (304,000 km) of ocean coastline—more than any other continent.

- If all the world's ice melted, the sea level would rise 200 to 300 feet (600—900 m).

- Each year, about 2.3 trillion gallons (8.74 trillion liters) of liquid waste are discharged directly into United States coastal waters.

- It is estimated that acid rain costs American farmers about $4 billion a year.

- The smallest drip from a leaky faucet can waste more than 50 gallons (190 liters) of water a day.

PLENTY OF PLANTS

Plants are an important part of our environment. Without plants, animals and human beings could not survive. Plants provide us with food, oxygen, medicines, building materials, seasonings, candy, drinks, industrial products, dyes, manufactured goods, paper, and decorations.

Plants are producers—the only living things able to make their own food. In order to grow, green plants use sunlight and store its energy in their leaves and stems. Sunlight enables plants to convert water—and also carbon dioxide, which all animals (including humans) give off as they breathe—into foods needed by the plant. This remarkable process is known as **photosynthesis.**

Plants are also responsible for producing oxygen—a gas necessary for animal survival. Plants add to the relative humidity of an area by releasing water vapor into the air. A plant's roots also help to reduce wind and water erosion by holding on to the soil, providing essential nutrients to other plants.

When the life cycle of plants is endangered by air pollution, when forests and plant life in certain areas are torn up or destroyed, or when poor farming methods are used, we are affected as well. Plants are a vital part of our daily lives and our survival.

Plant Requirements

Plants have certain needs for their growth and survival, just as we do.

Air To live, plants take two gases from the air. They use carbon dioxide, a natural product of animal life, to make food by the process of photosynthesis, and oxygen as fuel for the energy that helps them breathe.

Water To make their food, plants need water. Minerals in the water help plants to grow and replace damaged cells. Water is taken in through a plant's roots and is carried to the leaves.

Temperature Each plant variety requires a specific temperature range. Over many years, plants have adapted and learned to thrive where other plants could not survive. For example, a cactus or a palm tree could not live in the Arctic, where the cold temperatures would be harmful.

Sunlight Most plants, especially green leafy ones, need sunlight to grow. The light converts a plant's food into usable energy. But certain plants, such as mushrooms, don't like light and grow only in shady areas.

Soil Land plants need some type of soil in order to grow. It is usually a combination of organic material (decayed animal or vegetable matter, known as humus) and sand or clay. Soil helps hold the plant erect. Plants also get nutrients, or minerals, from the soil.

Hey, What's Inside?

Did you know that inside every seed is a very small plant waiting to grow? When the conditions are right, a new plant can begin life. What does it need?

You need:
dried lima beans
a container of water
a dinner knife
a magnifying glass

WHAT TO DO:

Soak several lima beans in a container of water overnight. The next day, choose some of the seeds and place them on a countertop or some paper. Ask an adult to use a knife to pry along the edge of the seed's coat (the hard covering of the seed) and open it up for you. (Knives, especially sharp ones, are dangerous and must be handled carefully.) When the two halves of the seed have separated, use your magnifying glass to examine the embryo in the seed (it will look like a miniature plant). You may want to look inside other seeds for their embryos, too.

WHAT HAPPENS:

You will be able to see the three basic parts of a seed—the seed coat, the food storage area, and the embryo.

WHY:

Many plants, such as lima beans, reproduce sexually—that is, a

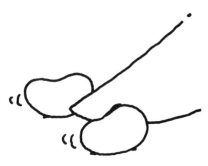

sperm cell from a male plant and an egg cell from a female plant combine in the flower of a plant and a seed begins to form. Inside the seed is a miniature plant called an embryo. There is also some food material in the seed so that a newly forming plant will have a ready food source as it begins its life. Covering the embryo and food source is a seed coat that serves as protection for the seed until the new plant is ready to start. Then, when the conditions are right (moisture and warmth), the seed **germinates**, or begins to grow. The embryo breaks out of the seed, like a chick out of an egg, and starts its life as a new plant.

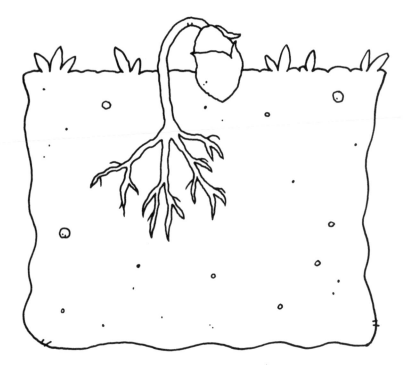

Help Me Out

Do you know what seeds need to begin growing? Here's how you can find out.

You need:

36 radish seeds
6 small sealable plastic bags
3 paper towels
safety scissors
water
bottle of nail polish
felt-tip marker

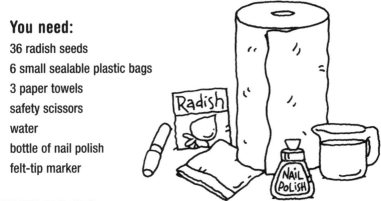

WHAT TO DO:

Label each small bag with a number. Cut each paper towel in half. Moisten four of the pieces, leaving one dry (you will not need the sixth piece). As directed below, place the towels in the bottoms of the bags. Drop six radish seeds into each bag and then finish setting up each bag as follows:

Bag 1: moist paper towel (water), no light (put in a drawer or closet), room temperature.

Bag 2: moist paper towel (water), light, room temperature.

Bag 3: dry paper towel (no water), light, room temperature.

Bag 4: no paper towel, water (seeds floating), light, room temperature.

Bag 5: moist paper towel (water), no light, keep in refrigerator or freezer.

Bag 6: moist paper towel (water), no light, room temperature, seeds covered by nail polish.

Record the date and time you began this activity and check each of the bags twice daily for any changes.

WHAT HAPPENS:

The seeds in **bag 1** and **bag 2** germinate (begin to grow). You may see some small difference in the seeds in **bag 4**. The seeds in the other bags do not start growing. What is wrong?

WHY:

Seeds need favorable temperature, enough moisture, and oxygen to germinate. Light is not needed for germination (the seeds, after all, usually germinate underground), but light is necessary later for growth. The seeds in **bag 6** can't get any air or moisture through the nail polish, so they don't germinate.

Swell Time

In order to begin the growing process, seeds need to take in water. Here's how they do it.

You need:

2 small sealable plastic bags
dry beans
water
container or tray

WHAT TO DO:

Fill each of the two bags with dry beans. Finish filling one of the bags with as much water as it can hold, then seal both bags and place them outside or on a tray in a sunny location.

WHAT HAPPENS:

After several hours, the seeds in the bag with the water begin to swell up. Eventually, the expanding seeds pop the bag open and seeds spill out all over the place.

WHY:

To begin the growing process, or sprout, seeds need to take in water. Water is absorbed through the skin of the seed (seed coat), and the seeds begin to expand. Because the bag had been filled with the dry seeds and now all the seeds in the bag were absorbing water and expanding, there wasn't enough room in the bag. So the expanding seeds forced the bag open and spilled out. In nature, seeds take in water and expand in the same way.

Top to Bottom

Plants need both roots and shoots in order to develop properly. To watch the growth of both plant parts at the same time, do this.

You need:

several large seeds
paper towel
string
water

2 small sheets of glass
or clear plastic (use saran wrap as sustitute)
a baking pan
bricks

WHAT TO DO:

Trim the blotting paper to fit the glass or plastic sheets. Wet the blotting paper well and lay it on top of one of the glass or plastic sheets. Arrange some seeds on the blotting paper, placing them at least 2 inches (5 cm) in from the edge. Put the other clear sheet on top. Tie the "seed sandwich" together securely with string and place it on edge in the pan. Support it upright, at an angle of about 45 degrees, with one or more bricks. Pour $1/_2$ inch (1 cm) or so of water into the pan. Add more when needed, to keep the blotting paper wet.

WHAT HAPPENS:

In a few days, the seeds will sprout, the shoots going up and the roots going down. Use a marker to make lines on the glass or a thin strip of masking tape to mark the daily or weekly growth of the seeds.

WHY:

The seeds sprout because you have provided them with water, light, and air. The roots always grow downward and the actual plant upward. Depending on the seeds used, you may see tiny leaves form. All seeds in nature demonstrate this same type of growth.

A Growing Enterprise

Some seeds are easy to grow, while others are more difficult. Fruit-bearing plants are very hard to grow from seed. That is why many fruit farmers use other ways to start growing new fruit trees, such as **grafts** (attaching a part of one plant to a part of another plant) or **root stocks** (sections of root).

To try growing some fruit plants at home (keep in mind, however, that the success rate is very low), you need some seeds. The easiest way to get them is to buy a couple of your favorite fruits—not the seedless variety! Take the seeds from the fruit, wash the seeds in water (don't use soap), and let them dry well in a warm place.

Some fruits you can try growing from seeds include apple, pear, pumpkin, orange, grape, cherry, peach, banana, fig, apricot, plum, quince, nectarine, lemon, lime, tomato, melon, persimmon, and grapefruit.

When you are ready to plant, get several small plastic cups and fill each one with some potting soil. Moisten the soil and plant four or five seeds from one of the fruits in each cup. Plant as many different varieties of fruit seed as possible and note which ones were the easiest to grow and which ones were the most difficult.

After you have sprouted one or more fruits and they have reached a height of 5 or 6 inches (12.5–15 cm), you may want to transplant them outdoors.

Hawaiian Harvest

Almost everybody loves the taste of pineapple. Now you can grow this delicious fruit in your own home.

Buy a whole pineapple. Have an adult cut off the crown of the pineapple (top part, with the green leaves) leaving about 1 to 2 inches (2.5–5 cm) of the fruit attached. Let the crown dry for thirty-six hours, then plant it in a large container with soil in a warm location–about 72°F (22°C) is ideal. Keep the soil evenly moist but not too wet.

Pineapple develops on top of a long stem that may need to be supported by sticks or secured upright with string when the fruit grows large. If no fruit develops, put the whole plant (with its container) inside a large plastic bag. Place a rotting apple or lemon inside the bag, close it up, and leave it for several days (the ethylene gas produced by the rotting fruit will help stimulate fruiting). Later, you may want to transplant the fruit to a larger container or, if you live where it is very warm, outside in loose, sandy soil.

Green Highways

Plants *must* be able to carry water and nutrients to all their parts in order to grow, but can you prove that they actually do it? Sure you can! Here's how.

You need:
a fresh stalk of celery
2 glasses of water
red food coloring
a dinner knife

WHAT TO DO:

Put the two glasses of water side by side. Place four drops of red food coloring into one of the glasses. Cut off the dried bottom end of the celery stalk and then cut the stalk up the middle from the bottom of the stalk to the leaves. Stand one half of the celery stalk in the glass with the clear water and the other in the glass with the red water. For the next several hours, go back every hour and check on your celery stalk experiment.

WHAT HAPPENS:

The celery in the glass of plain water shows no change, but telltale streaks of red move up the stalk of the celery standing in the colored water.

WHY:

All plants have special tubes in their stems that act something like drinking straws. These tubes move water, and the nutrients in it, from a plant's roots up into the leaves. Slight pressure differences in the tubes actually "pull" the water up the stalk, using a process called **osmosis**. This allows the plant to get the water and food needed for it to grow and develop. By putting red food coloring into the water, you are able to track the water's path up the stalk and prove your theory.

The Name Game

How would you like to spell your name with plants? Here's how.

Fill a large flat cake pan with soil. Smooth it over so that the soil is level and moisten it with water. Using a toothpick or the end of a knife, trace your name into the surface of the soil.

Open a packet of radish seeds and carefully plant the seeds in the grooves you made for the letters of your name. (Be sure to follow the directions for proper planting depth and distance between seeds given on the seed packet.) Cover the seeds with soil and place the pan in a sunny location and water occasionally. After a few days, the radishes will sprout into the shape of your name.

Later, you may want to write your name in plants again, using different varieties of seeds (grass seed and mung bean seeds work especially well).

Water In, Water Out

Plants take in water in order to grow, but they also give off water.

You need:

a small potted plant
a clear plastic bag
water
tape or string

WHAT TO DO:

Water the plant thoroughly. Place the plastic bag over the green, leafy part of the plant and close it up gently around the stem with tape or string. Place the plant in a sunny location for several hours.

WHAT HAPPENS:

Water droplets form on the inside of the bag.

WHY:

Plant leaves have tiny openings called **stomata** in them. In most plants, stomata are located on the underside of the leaves. During a plant's food-making process, air is taken in and released through these openings. Water, in the form of water vapor, is also released through the stomata into the atmosphere. You can see that water vapor as it condenses and forms water droplets on the inside of the plastic bag.

One of the reasons why a jungle is so humid is because of all the water vapor being released by the many trees and the vegetation in the area. The amount of water a plant loses varies with the weather conditions as well as the size and shape of its leaves.

Don't Crowd Me

Do plants like togetherness or wide-open spaces?

You need:

shoe box   potting soil
water   bean seeds

WHAT TO DO:

Fill the shoe box with potting soil. At one
end of the box, plant six bean seeds very
close together. At the other end of the box
plant six more seeds, but space them about $1^1/_2$ inches (4 cm)
apart. Water the soil thoroughly, being careful not to wash it
away from the seeds. Set the box aside and watch what happens
to the seeds. Record the number of seeds that sprout, and continue to grow, at each end of the box.

WHAT HAPPENS:

The side with the seeds planted closer together has fewer
sprouts, and they grow more slowly than the seeds planted far-
ther apart at the other end.

WHY:

Plants need space in order to grow properly. When plants are
crowded together, they have to compete for the limited
resources available. As a result, the sprouts may not get all the
soil nutrients, sunlight, and water they need to grow strong. To
achieve full growth, there must be enough space left between
plants. In nature, seeds are scattered over a large area, so quite
a number are able to sprout and grow in an uncrowded environment. This is why gardeners and farmers are very careful
not to plant their crops too close together.

Breathe Deeply

Do plants breathe? If so, how?

You need:

elodea plants
  (from the aquarium
  or pet store)
deep container
clear funnel
test tube

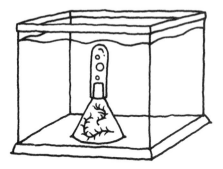

WHAT TO DO:

Fill the aquarium or container almost to the top with water. Place several elodea plants inside, close together in the middle, and cover them with the clear funnel (wide mouth over the plants and narrow neck pointing upward). Dip the test tube in the water, making sure that it fills with water. Then, still underwater, turn the test tube over onto the stem of the funnel, making sure no water escapes. Place the aquarium in a sunny location for a few days and watch what happens in the top of the test tube.

WHAT HAPPENS:

You will see oxygen building up in the top of the test tube (pushing out the water).

WHY:

The elodea plants (like other plants) produce oxygen. Because elodea are aquatic plants, this oxygen is released into the water, where it becomes available to organisms that need it, such as fish. In this experiment, the oxygen collects in the top of the test tube, replacing the water.

Follow That Light

Do plants always grow toward the light? Here's a great experiment to prove that they do.

You need:

2 shoe boxes
a healthy plant

WHAT TO DO:

Cut two corners of cardboard from one of the shoe boxes.
Tape the pieces inside the other shoe box as shown. Cut a hole in the top side. Place a healthy plant (a growing bean plant is fine) in the bottom and place the lid on the box. Put the closed shoe box in a sunny location. Every other day or so, remove the lid for a moment and quickly water the plant.

WHAT HAPPENS:

The plant grows toward the light source, even bending around the cardboard pieces to do it.

WHY:

All green plant life needs light in order to grow. Through a process known as **phototropism**, plants grow in whichever direction is toward the light. In your experiment, the plant grew toward the sunlight, even though the cardboard pieces were in the way. One of the reasons we turn our potted houseplants occasionally is so they will be able to get equal amounts of light on all sides and grow straight. If we did not, the plants would "lean" in the direction of the light.

Hanging On

The previous experiment showed how plants always grow toward a light source. This experiment will now demonstrate how powerful that process is.

You need:

a small potted plant
  with a strong root system
2 large sponges
string

WHAT TO DO:

Carefully remove the plant from its pot (try to leave as much soil around the roots as possible). Wet the two sponges, wrap them around the root system, and tie them together with string. Turn the plant upside down (roots upward) and hang it from the ceiling near a sunny window. Check the plant occasionally and keep the sponges moistened.

WHAT HAPPENS:

After a few days, the stem and top of the plant will turn and begin to grow upward toward the light.

WHY:

The leaves and stems of a plant will grow in the direction of a light source, following the process of phototropism, even if the plant is made to stand on its head! Also, a plant's roots will always grow downward, trying to reach the necessary nutrients in the soil.

See Me Grow

Have you ever wondered how plants grow under the ground? Here's a neat way to find out.

You need:

a shoe box
scissors
a variety of seeds
potting soil

clear acetate or plastic
 (from an office supply store)
masking tape
pebbles
water

WHAT TO DO:

Cut a section from the side of a strong shoe box, leaving about a 1-inch (2.5 cm) border all around. Tape the acetate inside, tight against the opening. Punch some small holes in the bottom of the box. Put in a layer of pebbles and fill the box with potting soil. Plant several seeds in the soil, placing them up against the acetate so you can see them behind the sheet. Water the seeds, then place the box outside or on a tray in the window. Watch the seeds for several days.

WHAT HAPPENS:

The seeds germinate and plants begin to grow. You can watch the shoots of the plant grow upward and the roots reach down.

WHY:

Plants need roots in order to take in water and other nutrients from the soil. They do this through tiny roots called root hairs. Roots generally grow in a downward direction to obtain the water and nutrients necessary for the plant's growth.

Flower Power

How can a little plant grow right up through a sidewalk?

You need:

any healthy potted plant

2 small boxes

paper clips

a sheet of clear acetate
  or plastic (from office supply store)

WHAT TO DO:

Put the potted plant on a sunny windowsill. Place the two boxes on either side of the pot (the boxes should be just a bit higher than the plant). Be careful not to shade the plant. Lay the clear plastic or acetate across the boxes. Make two identical "chains" of paper clips and lay them over the clear sheet so that the ends hang down the sides of the boxes. Arrange the chain ends evenly, and mark their positions on the sides of the boxes. Water and care for the plant as you would normally. Check the positions of the chains now and then.

WHAT HAPPENS:

As the plant grows, it pushes upward against the clear sheet. The rate of growth is measured by the markings made of the ends of the clip chains as they move up the sides of the boxes.

WHY:

Plants are incredibly strong. They are able to push up through the toughest soil as well as through rocks and cement to reach the light. This is why weeds can push up through the tiniest sidewalk cracks looking for sunlight—a necessary ingredient for their growth.

A Powerful Force

Plants often push their way up through even the tiniest crack in rocks or sidewalks, sometimes breaking up those hard objects. This is one way plants have of breaking apart large rocks into much smaller pebbles and stones.

You can see this for yourself. First, get some plaster of paris from a craft or hobby shop. Soak a few bean seeds in water overnight. The next day, plant two or three of them in a plastic cup filled with potting soil. Moisten the soil thoroughly.

Mix the plaster of paris according to the package directions, until it is like a thick milkshake. Pour a layer of the mixture, about $1/4$ inch (0.5 cm) thick, on top of the soil in the cup. Put the cup in a sunny location and watch what happens (if you use a clear plastic cup and plant the seeds near the sides, you will be able to look through and watch the growth process). You will probably see the developing bean plants push up and through the plaster of paris—just like weeds are able to push up and through small cracks in a sidewalk.

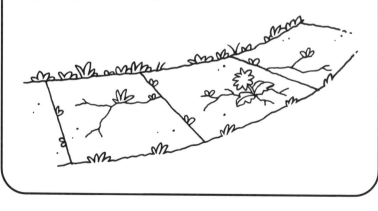

Hold That Mold

Would you believe that there are millions of plants growing right in your kitchen?

You need:

3 slices of white bread
3 small sealable plastic bags
water
magnifying glass

WHAT TO DO:

Take two slices of bread and wet them lightly (don't soak them). Carefully rub one slice across a kitchen table or counter-top (do it gently so you don't tear the bread). Place the slice of bread in a plastic bag and seal it. Then take the second moistened slice and gently rub it over the surface of the kitchen floor. Put it in a second bag and seal it. Now, place the third (dry) slice of bread in the third bag and seal it. Place all three bags in a closet or other dark place for a couple of days.

WHAT HAPPENS:

You find mold growing on the surfaces of the two slices of bread that were moistened, rubbed over the kitchen surfaces, and placed in the bags. There may be some mold on the dry slice, too (some bakeries use preservatives to keep their breads fresh longer). Try this experiment with other types of bread (wheat, rye), or rub slices over other surfaces (wall, sidewalk).

WHY:

Molds and other microscopic plants are everywhere. In order to grow they need special conditions, such as moisture, warmth, and darkness instead of light.

My Bud-Bud-Buddy

Yeast is a plant used by cooks and bakers. The way it grows makes it a very special plant.

You need:

2 packets dry yeast

2 small sealable plastic bags

1 teaspoon (5 mL) sugar

1 cup (240 mL) lukewarm water

WHAT TO DO:

Put $1/_2$ cup (120 mL) lukewarm water in each of the bags and add the contents of one yeast packet to each bag. Put the spoonful of sugar into one bag. Close both bags, squeezing out as much air as possible before sealing them. Shake the bags well for a minute, then place them in a warm or sunny location.

WHAT HAPPENS:

The bag with just the water and yeast shows little change. But the bag with the water, yeast, and sugar has changed a lot. Bubbles have formed inside, and the bag is swelling up!

WHY:

Yeast is a microorganism that needs food in order to grow well. Sugar is a good food source for yeast. Yeast grows by producing one or more bumps, or buds, that break off and become new yeast plants. As it grows, yeast also produces carbon dioxide gas. It is often added to bakery products, such as cake or bread, to make the dough rise. Without yeast, breads would be very flat.

All living things need food in order to grow and survive. This is true for both simple plants, such as yeast, and more complex plants, such as redwood trees; they all need nutrients.

Adopt a Tree

Trees are some of the most beautiful plants in the world. Some are also so common that people don't even notice them. Here's an activity to help you learn more about one special tree.

You need:

string   a measuring tape
plastic bags   drawing paper
pencil and crayons   your journal

WHAT TO DO:

Select a tree near where you live. If possible, locate a deciduous tree (one that sheds its leaves each year). The tree should be in a place that is easy to reach, because you will be visiting your tree for the next twelve months. To start, draw a picture of your tree (or photograph it) and write down in your journal any unusual markings, characteristics, or patterns you notice. Measure 3 feet (90 cm) up the tree trunk from the ground and tie a piece of string around the tree at that point. Measure the section of string to determine the circumference of the tree (how big around it is). Collect some of the tree's leaves and save them in small plastic bags. Place a piece of paper against the bark of the tree and rub a crayon over the paper until the pattern of the bark appears. What other kinds of learning activities can you do with your "adopted" tree?

WHAT HAPPENS:

Trees change during the year. They grow, shed their leaves, grow new leaves, serve as a home for all types of animal life, and contribute to the balance of nature in your local community.

WHY:

Since you will be focusing your attention on this one tree for a period of one year, you will undoubtedly notice many changes that you had never even seen or thought of before with all other trees. Even one tree can have an influence on the environment in your small corner of the world.

Plants Breathe, Too

What do you think happens to plants if there are lots of pollutants in the air? Let's find out.

You need:

3 bean plants (may be grown from seed)
petroleum jelly
measuring tape or ruler
drawing paper
coloring pencils

WHAT TO DO:

Place the plants on a windowsill so they will all get the same amount of sunlight. Label the plants A, B, and C. Draw a picture of each plant and measure and record its height. Rub some petroleum jelly on the *top* side of all the leaves on plant A and on the *bottom* side of all the leaves on plant B. Leave plant C as it is. Water the plants every so often, as you normally would. Every other day, record the height of each plant and draw pictures of any changes that have taken place.

WHAT HAPPENS:

Plant C shows the most growth. Plant A shows less growth. Plant B shows little growth and begins to die.

WHY:

Clean air is necessary for the chemical reaction called **photosynthesis** (when a plant produces its own food) to occur. The air enters the plant through the stomata on the underside of the leaves. When the air is polluted or when the leaves are covered by something (such as petroleum jelly) that acts as a pollutant, photosynthesis cannot take place and the plant dies.

I'm Impressed!

Preserve the flowers and leaves you collect by using a simple plant press. *Get help to make this one.*

You need:

use of hand or machine drill

2 sheets of plywood or fiberboard, 10 by 13 inches (25 x 33 cm)

pieces of cardboard the size of a sheet of paper

white construction paper

4 long bolts with wing nuts

WHAT TO DO:

Ask an adult to drill holes (to fit your bolts) in each corner of the two sections of wood. The hole should be about 1 inch (2.5 cm) in from the top and side of each corner (if you drill the two boards together, the holes will be sure to match).

To use the press, put the connecting bolts through one board and lay it down so that the bolts stick upward. Lay a piece of cardboard on top of this board. Next, place a sheet of paper on top of the cardboard, and whatever you want to press (a flower or leaves) on top of the paper. Put another sheet of paper on top of the specimen, and then another piece of cardboard. Repeat this process, making plant material "sandwiches," until you have a stack of several cardboard pieces. Put the second piece of plywood on top of the last cardboard piece on the stack, threading the bolts through the holes. Put a wing nut on each bolt and tighten them until you feel pressure. Then carefully tighten each bolt in turn as much as you can, putting even pressure on the stack. The specimens will be pressed flat and will dry within a few weeks (check them occasionally if you wish). Later, you may want to glue your pressed plants onto sheets of colorful construction paper and place them in paper frames from a hobby or arts and crafts store for display around your home.

WHAT HAPPENS:

The wooden press you made puts pressure on the plant specimens placed in it and keeps them flat. The pressure is gentle but constant. Any "juices" squeezed from the plant material are absorbed by the white paper, so the plant dries out rapidly.

WHY:

People have been collecting and pressing plants, flowers, and leaves for many years. These pressings have been used in decorative displays and are a way of preserving some of nature's beauty long after a plant would normally die.

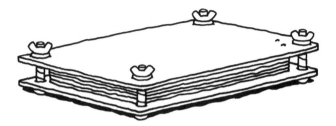

DID YOU KNOW?

- The leaves of a Venus flytrap can close over an insect in less than half a second.

- The giant sequoia tree does not begin to flower until it is at least 175 to 200 years old.

- The roots of a redwood tree are capable of holding more than 130,000 gallons (494,000 liters) of water.

- There are more than 250,000 species of flowering plants in the world.

- Pacific giant kelp can grow more than 17 inches (43 cm) a day and may reach lengths of up to 200 feet (90 m).

- Bamboo may grow as much as 3 feet (90 cm) each day.

- An average apple tree will lose up to 20 quarts (19 liters) of water a day through its leaves.

- The plant life of the oceans makes up about 85 percent of all greenery on the planet.

- Tree ring thickness is a good record of earthquakes.

- In tropical rain forests, certain plants known as epiphytes grow on the highest branches of trees. They have no roots and get their water and nutrients directly from the humid air.

- A mature saguaro cactus may weight up to 10 tons— and 80 percent of that weight is water.

- The largest seed in the world is the coconut.

- Lemons have more sugar in them than melons or peaches do, yet they are more sour because they contain more acid.

WONDERFUL WILDLIFE

Do you have a pet at home? Have you been to a zoo or an aquarium? Have you seen birds flying overhead, bees buzzing in the summertime, or snakes slithering through the grass? No doubt you have seen many kinds of animals where you live, for animals are a part of all our lives, and an important part of the world of nature, too.

Humans have always been fascinated by animals. We keep animals as pets, and we observe animals in special places such as zoos and wildlife parks. But it is important to remember that animals are affected by the actions of humans. If we throw garbage into a stream, the fish and insects are affected; if we destroy nests and burrows during construction projects, those animals can no longer live there; if we pollute the air, birds—in fact, all *breathing* animals—are affected. In other words, humans affect the survival of every living thing.

Learning about the wildlife in your area of the world will help you to appreciate the rich variety of animals that surround you—and which look to you to help keep them safe.

Feathered Friends

Birds are important members of every environment and they are fun to watch. Here's how to attract more birds to your house.

You need:

a clean plastic milk container
wild-bird seed
some strong string

WHAT TO DO:

Have an adult cut a panel from the side of the milk container, leaving a border around the opening. Tie the string tightly around the top, fill the container with some birdseed, and hang the new feeder in a nearby tree so you can see it from your window. Watch the birds that visit the feeder. What types of birds come to eat? How many, and at what time of day? Record your observations in the journal.

WHAT HAPPENS:

The feeder, if kept filled with food they like, attracts all kinds of birds. A book will help to identify the species, or types, of birds that live near you. You may learn to recognize certain individual birds that return often.

WHY:

Birds are affected by climate, and by the availability of food. They **adapt**, or get used to, an environment and will stay as long as they have the food, water, and shelter they need in order to live and raise their young. Offering them clean water (a birdbath), a birdhouse, and pieces of string and hair during nesting season are ways to encourage birds to stay nearby.

Well Fed

In cold weather, birds need to eat fat to maintain their body temperature. Here's how to help.

You need:

fat, lard, or suet
  (from butcher or supermarket)
a heavy pot
birdseed
a tin can
a nail and hammer
3 feet (90 cm) of string
can-size circle of cardboard

WHAT TO DO:

Have an adult melt the fat or suet in a heavy pot. *(Be very careful of spatters; hot fat can cause bad burns.)* Then add birdseed (twice as much seed as fat) to the liquid fat and stir carefully. Let it cool and thicken slightly.

Carefully, using a hammer and nail, punch a small hole in the middle of the can bottom (an adult can help here, too) and the cardboard circle. Thread the string through the hole in the can and out the top. Pour the soft seed mixture into the can (if it is too liquid, you may have to seal the hole). When the fat has hardened, gently remove the can and push the string through the cardboard. Knot the string, then tie your seed feeder to a nearby tree and watch the birds that visit it. (Experiment with other containers for differently shaped feeders.)

Feed Me, I'm Yours!

With a little imagination, you can create bird feeders from almost anything in your home. Here are five ideas to get you started. Place them outside and watch what happens. How many other bird feeders can you create?

1. Cut a half circle from the plastic lid of a coffee can. Nail or tape a small board to the side of the can and put some seed inside. Put the lid back on, so that it covers the bottom half, and lay the feeder outside.

2. Cut an orange in half. Scoop out the insides and make four small holes around the edge. Tie pieces of string to the holes around the orange half, fill it with seed, and hang it in a tree or bush.

3. Tie a string to a pinecone. Fill the crevices in the cone with peanut butter and roll the cone in some birdseed. Hang the cone from a tree branch.

4. Tie some unsalted peanuts onto various lengths of string. Hang these in a tree.

5. Tie a string to the stem of an apple. Roll the apple in some fat or bacon grease and then roll it in some birdseed. Hang it from a tree branch.

Woodside Restaurant

Here's a great feeder for you to make for your feathered friends. Fill it with your own homemade nourishing treat or this book's super recipe for World's Greatest Bird Food and they will enjoy it all year long.

Find a piece of wood 12–15 inches (30–40 cm) long and about 2 inches (5 cm) square. Ask an adult to drill a number of holes in the wood with a 1-inch (2.5 cm) drill bit, staggering the holes down each side. The holes should be about $3/4$ inch (2 cm) deep. Fasten an eye screw to one end of the stick and pass a long piece of strong string through it. Stuff the holes of the feeder with some sticky type of bird food mixture, then hang the feeder in a nearby tree. Place it at least 4 feet (125 cm) off the ground so that the birds who come to eat will be safe from cats. Watch to see who comes to visit.

Remember to put fresh food in the holes every so often to keep your Woodside Restaurant open for business and its feathered customers happy and coming back for more.

World's Greatest Bird Food

This nourishing recipe will keep birds coming back to your feeder all year—but especially in the winter.

Ingredients:

suet, from butcher or supermarket

a large frying pan

1 cup each chunky peanut butter, chopped nuts, sunflower seeds, and cornmeal

1 tablespoon crushed eggshells

WHAT TO DO:

With the help of an adult, cut the suet into small pieces and melt it slowly in a large frying pan. *(Be very careful of spatters; hot fat can cause bad burns.)* Measure 1 cup (240 mL) of melted fat. Let the melted fat cool until it becomes solid, then reheat it again and allow the liquid fat to cool off once more.

Thoroughly mix all of the other ingredients into the soft suet. Spoon the mixture into small plastic containers and put them in the refrigerator. When the mixture is firm, spoon some of it into the feeder holes of the Woodside Restaurant or some other bird feeder. Keep the remainder of the mixture refrigerated until needed.

Note:

Because of the cost or availability, you may want to experiment with different quantities or ingredients—for example, mixing together just peanut butter and sunflower seeds during the summer months, and adding the suet (for extra fat) only during the wintertime.

Home Sweet Home

Some of the best "builders" in the animal kingdom are birds. Let's find out how they do it.

You need:
binoculars
tweezers
a magnifying glass

WHAT TO DO:

In late fall or early winter, take your binoculars outside to look for one or more empty bird nests. If, when you find one, it is high up, ask an adult to get it down for you. Be sure that there are no eggs in the nest! Try to keep the nest as intact as possible. At home, use tweezers to carefully separate the pieces making up the nest. Examine them closely with the magnifying glass. Make a list of what was used to build the nest.

WHAT HAPPENS:

You will see that nests are constructed of many different types of materials, including twigs, grasses, straw, string, leaves, hair, feathers, and other things. You will also notice that the size and shape of nests vary depending on the species of bird that built it.

WHY:

Birds build their nests in different ways and using different materials. The construction of a nest depends largely on what material is available and how the eggs and young birds need to be protected while they are in the nest. As you continue to examine the nests of different species of birds you will notice many different variations in nest construction.

Look, Ma, No Hands!

Can you imagine how difficult it is to build a nest from things like twigs, grass, and feathers that you might find lying on the ground?

You need:
twigs   dried grasses
yarn   scraps of paper

WHAT TO DO:

Take a walk around your neighborhood or park and locate several different bird's nests. Look carefully at how the nests are constructed (be careful not to disturb any occupants). Using the materials listed above (and any others you think might help you—but no glue), try to build a bird's nest. Work with just your two hands and make a round nest that has room for two or three eggs.

WHAT HAPPENS:

You'll discover that nest building is not as easy as it may look. Hmmm, those birds must be smart!

WHY:

Birds are able to construct their nests with just their feet and beaks. Most birds seem to have learned the construction process by only seeing—from the inside—what their parents once built!

It's amazing to think that bird's nests are some of the most complicated homes in the animal kingdom—homes that are able to withstand bad weather and protect young birds as they grow and develop. So the next time anyone calls you a birdbrain, be sure to thank that person for the compliment.

Creepy Crawlies

What do snails do? What do snails eat? How do snails travel?
Here's how to discover the answers to those questions.

You need:

live land snails
pieces of lettuce
black construction paper
large wide-mouthed jar
damp soil
magnifying glass
cheesecloth
string or rubber band

WHAT TO DO:

Find some land snails from around your home (look in the moist soil of gardens in the early morning hours). Put a 2-inch (5 cm) layer of damp soil in the jar and place the snails in it. Place some cheesecloth over the jar opening and fasten it down securely with string or a rubber band to keep the occupants inside (snails can crawl up glass).

Sprinkle the soil every so often to keep it wet. Keep the jar in a cool, shady place. Put in some pieces of lettuce every so often. You will be able to keep and observe the behavior of the snails for several days.

Move one or more of the snails to a sheet of black construction paper to see it better. Place a snail in the middle of the sheet and surround it with bits of food—a slice of apple, a lettuce leaf, a piece of celery, some cereal—and watch what happens.

WHAT HAPPENS:

The snails leave trails behind them on the paper as they slowly move toward the kind of food they prefer. Did you turn one over to see how it moves over the paper?

WHY:

As snails travel, using their sole foot to push them along, they leave a trail of mucus behind them. This mucus protects them from sharp rocks and other harmful objects they travel over in their environment. (A snail can even travel over a razor blade without hurting itself.) Most snails enjoy eating food that has a lot of moisture, such as fresh leaves and other vegetation. That is why they are considered a pest by home gardeners.

Worm World

Would you be surprised to learn that earthworms are some of the most useful animals to human life? Be prepared to be surprised.

You need:

large wide-mouthed jar

tin can

gravel or small pebbles

soil

5 or 6 earthworms (from your garden, the bait shop, or the pet store)

dark construction paper

WHAT TO DO:

Stand the tin can in the middle of the jar. Place a layer of gravel or small pebbles about $1/_2$ inch (1.5 cm) deep on the bottom of the jar, between the can and the jar sides. Fill the jar with garden soil up to the height of the tin can. Place the worms on top of the soil.

Wrap the dark construction paper around the outside of the jar to keep out the light. (Note: Check the condition of the soil every so often and moisten it as needed.)

WHAT HAPPENS:

The worms will begin burrowing into the soil. After several days, they will have dug a series of tunnels. You will be able to see these tunnels by carefully removing the construction paper from the sides of the jar. (Replace the construction paper after observing their work so the worms will continue to tunnel in the darkness.) You should be able to watch the worms' behavior, without harming them, for three or four weeks, but then you should put them back outside.

WHY:

Worms feed by taking soil through their bodies, creating tunnels as they go. These tunnels **aerate** the soil, providing plants with the oxygen they need to grow. If it weren't for earthworms, many varieties of plants would not be able to survive. Farmers consider earthworms some of the best friends they have.

The Ants Go Marching . . .

You may not want to invite ants to your next picnic, but here's a way to invite them to your house for a short visit.

You need:

large clear jar

loose or sandy soil, with ants

water

sugar water (2–3 large spoonfuls of
 sugar dissolved in a cup of water)

small shovel or trowel

black construction paper

a small saucer

large cake pan

small bits of fruit

WHAT TO DO:

Look outside for a rotting piece of wood, which ants love, or an area with lots of ants. Scoop up into the glass jar some of the soil nearby, along with a healthy collection of ants. Put the lid on until you get the ants home. Cover the jar with black construction paper so that it is completely dark inside. Put some water in the cake pan, put the saucer upside down in the middle of it, and place the jar on the upturned saucer before removing the lid (the water prevents the ants from escaping from the jar). Sprinkle some sugar water over the soil and place two or three small bits of fruit inside.

WHAT HAPPENS:

The ants begin to dig tunnels in the soil. If it is dark enough, they will dig their tunnels next to the sides of the glass. If you remove the black construction paper every week or so, you can see the progress they have made in their tunnel building.

WHY:

Many kinds of ants live in large colonies underground. Each of the ants has a job to do in order to keep the colony running smoothly. Worker ants are responsible for building the tunnels and the small caves that are home to the ant colony. It is in these tunnels that all the ants in a colony live, work, sleep, and eat.

Did you know that there are more than twelve thousand varieties of ants in the world?

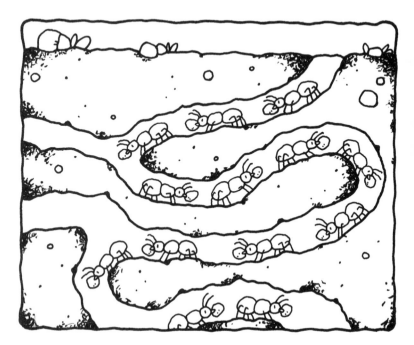

Cricket Critters

You may have never thought of keeping crickets as house pets, but in some countries, such as Japan, they are valued members of the household.

You need:

an empty oatmeal box
a sheer nylon stocking (light color)
markers or poster paints
dry soil
twigs
a bottle cap
a small bowl
a cardboard tube from a roll of toilet paper
shredded paper
crickets (from the pet store)
bran or oatmeal cereal
apple or potato slice

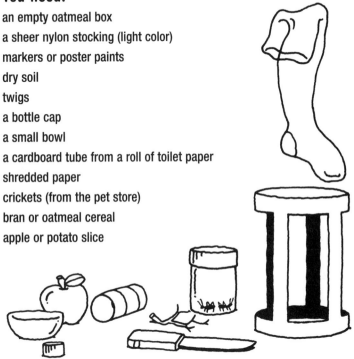

WHAT TO DO:

Draw large "windows" on the sides of the empty round box. Leave frames around the windows as shown. Have an adult cut out the windows using a sharp knife (this can be very hard to do and you might get hurt, so *don't* do it yourself). Remove the remaining label from the box and decorate the outside with poster paint or markers.

Place the small bowl in the "cage." Fill the bottom of the box, and the bowl, with dry soil until you can just see the rim of the bowl. Push the bottle cap, open end up, into the soil until the rim is nearly level with the soil. Carefully pull the nylon stocking up over the box. Put shredded paper and the cardboard tube in the cage. Water the soil in the bowl and keep it moist. Fill the bottle cap with fresh water for drinking. Put in six or seven crickets and close up the top of the stocking to keep the critters in. The crickets can be easily cared for by feeding them some bran or oatmeal cereal, keeping the bottle cap filled with fresh water, and occasionally placing a slice of apple or potato in the cage.

WHAT HAPPENS:

The crickets thrive in this miniature environment. The females lay their eggs in the moist soil of the bowl (be sure the soil is always damp). If you're lucky, you'll see the cricket eggs hatch into small crickets (called nymphs) and grow into adults in about eight weeks.

WHY:

Crickets enjoy simple surroundings. As long as they have a constant food supply and some moisture they will thrive in almost any environment. (Note: When you get your crickets from the pet store, be sure you have both males and females. Crickets look the same, except that females have a long slender rod, called an **ovipositor**, protruding from their back end. They use this ovipositor to lay their eggs.)

Web Warriors

Spiderwebs come in all shapes and sizes. Here's how you can preserve a few.

You need:

clear plastic adhesive sheets
  (from the hardware or variety store)

masking tape

black construction paper

hair spray

WHAT TO DO:

Taking hair spray, masking tape, and black construction paper, go outside and find a spiderweb nearby (make sure the spider isn't at home). Make five rings of masking tape, sticky side outward, around the fingers of one hand. Press the construction paper against the tape rings so that the paper sticks to them and to your hand. (Now you can hold the construction paper vertically and it won't fall.) Carefully place the hand with the construction paper just behind the spiderweb. With your other hand, gently spray the web from the front with hair spray, so that the spray pushes the web against the construction paper.

Slowly and gently (the web is fragile), move the web stuck on the construction paper away from where it is attached. When you get home, place a clear plastic adhesive sheet over the web and construction paper and around the back. (Note: This takes practice, so don't get discouraged if everything doesn't work out quite right the first time around.) Collect several different kinds of spiderwebs this way and compare them.

WHAT HAPPENS:

When you use the hair spray, the spiderweb is pushed against the construction paper and sticks to it. The adhesive plastic sheet seals the web against the paper. If the sheeting covers the back of the construction paper as well, the specimen is airtight, so it is preserved and doesn't get damaged.

WHY:

Spiderwebs are as varied as the number of spiders in the world. Spiders use their webs for homes and to help them collect the food they need to survive. When insects and other tiny animals become trapped in the threads of a spiderweb, they are food for the web's owner. Spiders also "wrap" trapped insects to eat later.

A spiderweb in the early morning, with dew glistening on its threads, is one of the most beautiful sights in nature.

Net Gain

Here's a handy insect net to help you capture some of the bugs that fly or jump by.

You need:

a wire coat hanger

a wooden pole
4 feet (125 cm) long and about
2 inches (5 cm) in diameter

duct tape

flexible tape measure

nylon netting
(use pantyhose
as substitute)

scissors

a strip of cotton fabric
2 inches (5 cm) wide

needle and strong thread

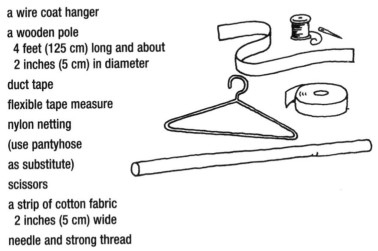

WHAT TO DO:

Shape the triangle part of the hanger into a circle, and straighten the hook. Tape the straightened hook to the end of the pole with the duct tape.

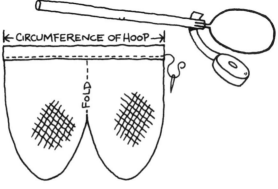

Using the measuring tape, measure the circumference (distance around) the wire circle. Cut the nylon netting into the shape shown here, making the straight edge the same length as the measurement around the wire loop. Sew the cotton strip to the straight edge of the net, and then sew the side seams. Attach the net to the hoop by folding the cotton strip over the wire frame and sewing it to itself.

Use your insect net to collect various types of bugs, but stay away from bees or wasps or you could be stung! When you catch something, twist the handle quickly to close the net and trap the insect inside. (You may have to practice with the net awhile to learn how to close it fast enough.)

WHAT HAPPENS:

You'll be able to capture a wide variety of flying insects with your nature collector's net. You may want to keep some insects for a few days to examine them—noting their body shapes, behavior, and what they eat—before releasing them again.

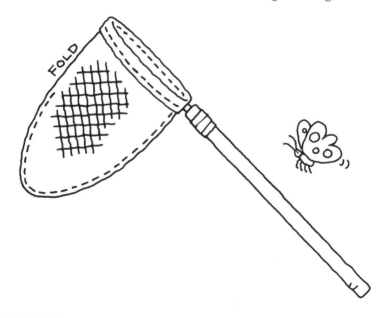

Mealworm Magic

Here's an animal you don't think about much, but you can keep it in your home for a good while and maybe see some strange things.

You need:

20 to 25 mealworms (from the pet store)
a plastic shoe box (from the variety or department store)
bran
flour
bread
apples

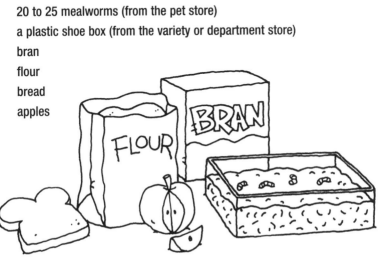

WHAT TO DO:

Fill the plastic shoe box about two-thirds full with a mixture of bran, flour, and small pieces of bread. Place the mealworms in the box and put on the cover. Lift the cover every few days, or have an adult drill several small holes in the lid to let some air in. Keep the box in a warm location—between 75 and 80° F (24 and 26° C). Put in a slice of apple and replace it with a fresh piece every few days.

WHAT HAPPENS:

That depends on how long you keep and watch your mealworms and just how old they are.

WHY:

The mealworm is the larval stage (part of the life cycle) of the darkling beetle. The **larvae**, which are young mealworms, grow for about six months. They then turn into **pupae**, a stage that lasts for about three weeks. Afterward, the adult beetles emerge from the cocoon. The cycle is then repeated (male and female beetles mate, eggs are laid, the eggs hatch into mealworms, the mealworms turn into pupae, the pupae turn into adult beetles). You can watch each stage of insect growth (egg, larvae, pupae, adult) by looking through the sides of the plastic box or carefully sifting through the bran mixture with your fingers. The bran provides the nourishment these animals need, and the apple slices provide the necessary moisture.

Mealworms are raised primarily to serve as a food source for other animals (lizards and salamanders love them). They are a big part of many environments, living deep within the soil. By adding to the bran mixture and replacing dried-out apple slices, you can keep your colony of mealworms for some time. Later, you may want to release them to a new home—a warm and moist area near a rotting log, for example.

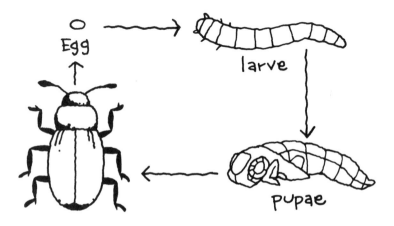

Bee Home, Be Careful

Bee stings can be dangerous, but bees are important to the environment. Here's how to help them survive.

You need:
25 large drinking straws
masking tape
modeling clay
string

WHAT TO DO:
Plug up one end of each straw with modeling clay. Mix up the straws so that some plugged ends face one way and some the other. Tape the bundle together tightly. With string or tape, fasten it sideways (horizontally) underneath a windowsill, rain gutter, or the roof overhang of your house (if high up, have an adult help you place the straw bundle). The bundle must be in a sunny location.

WHAT HAPPENS:
Bees may move into their new "home" and set up housekeeping. You'll see them coming and going.

WHY:
A bee's nest is full of small cells and tunnels. They use these to care for their young and to store the honey they make. Your "straw hive" offers the bees a place that is very similar to their regular hives. However, depending on where you live, the time of the year (early spring is best), and the type of bees that live in your area, you may or may not be able to attract bees to your nests. Some varieties of bees are very particular about where they live.

Sea Shrimp at the Seashore

Brine shrimp, though tiny, are some of the most amazing animals! Let's grow some.

You need:

brine shrimp eggs (from the pet store)
kosher or noniodized salt
2-quart (2 liter) pot or container
water
teaspoon
medicine dropper
hand lens or
  inexpensive microscope
water

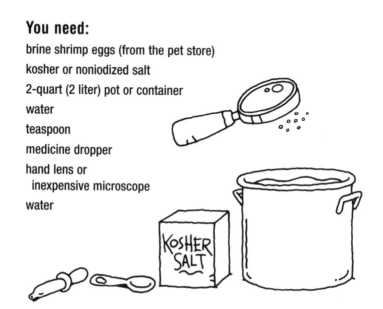

WHAT TO DO:

Fill the pot with 2 quarts (2 liters) of water and allow it to sit for three days, stirring it occasionally. (Most city water has chlorine in it, which would kill the shrimp. By letting it "age" for a while, the chlorine gas can escape from the water.) Dissolve 5 teaspoons (25 mL) of noniodized salt into the water. Add $1/2$ teaspoon (2.5 mL) of brine shrimp eggs to the salt water and place the pot in a warm spot. Each day use the medicine dropper to remove a few eggs from the water and observe them with your hand lens or microscope. You can draw a series of illustrations in your journal to record the growth of your brine shrimp.

WHAT HAPPENS:

The brine shrimp eggs begin to hatch in about two days. They will continue to grow in the water until they reach their adult stage. You can watch this growth process over a period of many days.

WHY:

The brine shrimp eggs you can buy at the pet store are dried so that they can be stored for very long periods of time (especially when kept in a dry place). When these eggs are placed in salt water, however, they "wake up" and begin to grow. Although they are very small, you can watch them grow for many days. (Note: Brine shrimp eggs are sold as food for aquarium fish.)

Can't See Me!

In order to survive, smaller animals sometimes need to hide from larger ones. One way that certain animals avoid being seen, and protect themselves from being eaten, is to use protective coloring, or camouflage. These animals match their body color to the colors in their environment so that they blend in and almost disappear.

You need:
100 green and 100 red toothpicks
(from the party store or grocery store)
watch or stopwatch

WHAT TO DO:

Ask a friend to mix up all 200 toothpicks and spread them out over a certain area of grass (your front lawn or a section of a park, for example). The area should be about 25 yards (25 m) square. As you pick up the toothpicks, have your partner time you for one minute, two minutes, and three minutes. Put the found toothpicks aside in bunches each time.

WHAT HAPPENS:

After several minutes, you probably notice that you are finding and picking up more red toothpicks than green toothpicks. Later, you can count the red and the green toothpicks you found, and record in your journal the exact number of each color you found during each period.

WHY:

Because the green toothpicks were closer to the color of the test environment (the green grass) than the red ones, the green ones were harder to see and find. Animals that are able to blend into their environment have a better chance for survival than those who have colors that make them easy to see. The ability of animals to match the colors of their surroundings, or use camouflage, helps them to protect themselves. Green lizards are able to hide better in an area with lots of green shrubs and plants than would red or yellow lizards. **Predators** (animals that hunt and would eat them) have a more difficult time locating them.

Find Me if You Can

Camouflage is the ability of an organism (plant or animal) to blend with its surroundings. In doing so, the organism is able to escape detection and "hide" in certain parts of its environment. The katydid, for example, is an insect that looks like a leaf, making it hard to see in a plant or tree. Because of their dull color, certain types of caterpillars look like bird droppings when they roll up, so they do it when danger is near, to avoid being eaten by birds and other enemies. Some types of spiders have features that look like the parts of a flower. By sitting on a flower, they can avoid being a predator's next meal. Desert plants called **lithops** resemble small rocks in shape and color and so avoid being chewed for their moisture. It is only when water is easily available that they bloom to spread their pollen.

Mimicry, the ability of one species to imitate the coloring or behavior of another, is also a form of protection. Some small animals or insects are unpleasant-tasting or dangerous, so larger animals avoid them. To survive, other animals and insects have evolved to look like the dangerous ones, with similar colors and body movements. By pretending to be what they're not, these copycats are left alone and live longer lives. One type of fly, for example, looks like a dangerous and poisonous wasp; one very tasty butterfly looks just like a bad-tasting moth; and one caterpillar has body markings that make it look like the eyes of a giant bird.

Track Record

Animals leave tracks wherever they go. Here's how you can record those tracks.

You need:

large milk carton,
  top and bottom removed,
  remainder cut horizontally
  into 1-inch (2.5 cm) strips

old bowl or pot

plaster of paris

water

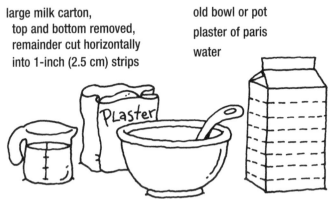

WHAT TO DO:

Find an animal track or print in some soft dirt or mud (it can be a cat or dog track, or maybe a deer or some other wild animal in your area). Put a milk carton square around the track and push it partway down into the soil. Be careful not to disturb the track. Mix the plaster of paris and water together in an old bowl or pot according to the directions on the package, until it is like a thick milkshake. Pour it into the mold up to the top of the cardboard strip. Wait for about an hour until the plaster cast hardens. Remove the cast from the ground print and take off the cardboard strip.

WHAT HAPPENS:

You now have a cast of the foot of the animal that made the print. You may want to make casts of several different animals tracks for display.

WHY:

When animals walk on damp ground, they leave impressions of their feet, just as we do. By studying these tracks, we can tell a lot about the animals, how they were moving, and perhaps even why they were moving the way they were. If the track is very deep, the animals may have been very heavy. If the track is deeper at the front of the print than at the back, the animal was walking rapidly (or even running). If the depths of the four tracks (of a four-footed animal) are uneven, the animal may be limping from an old injury or may be hurt.

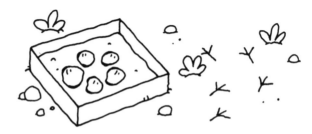

I'm All Yours!

"Adopt" an endangered animal. Write to the American Zoo and Aquarium Association and ask about their animal adoption program. (Ask a parent first.) For a few dollars, you will be assigned an endangered animal and receive a photograph and a fact sheet about your "adoptee." The money you send will be used to feed and care for the animal.

Share this project with your teacher and classmates. By collecting money or contributing small amounts each, your entire class can adopt an endangered animal and learn all about it.

Sound Off

You may be surprised to discover the wide variety of animal sounds you can find in your neighborhood.

You need:
a tape recorder with a microphone on a long cord
a broom handle or long pole
masking tape

WHAT TO DO:

Tape the microphone handle to the end of the pole or broom (be sure not to put tape over the microphone itself). Go outside on a clear and calm day and place the microphone near one or more wildlife homes (a bird's next, bee-hive, or wasp's nest, for example). It helps if you know the animals are at home, but be careful.

You can either hold the micro-phone on the pole near the ani-mal's home or stick the pole into the ground. Take care doing this so that you do not disturb any birds or animals nearby. (It may be a good idea to have an adult along, especially if you're dealing with bees or wasps.) Turn on the micro-phone and record the sounds and noises the animals make.

Don't forget to make some field notes for your nature journal about the types or numbers of animals you see and have been able to catch on tape.

WHAT HAPPENS:

Your nature recordings will help you discover the many different sounds that the animals in your neighborhood make. (Note: It's important to make your recordings on calm days, since microphones often pick up wind sounds that will mask the sounds animals may make.) Collect the neighborhood animal sounds and combine them with photographs, illustrations, and field notes on the behavior and habits of the animal. These data can be collected into an attractive notebook or display box for sharing with friends and family.

WHY:

Animals such as birds and insects make all different kinds of sounds as they go about their daily chores. Some of the sounds they make are used to "talk" to others of their species, some are for protection, some to help locate mates, and some sounds they make can call others to a food source or tell them where food can be found nearby.

DID YOU KNOW?

- The roundworm lives for only 12 days; the lake sturgeon (a fish) can live more than 150 years.

- Crickets have hearing organs in their knees.

- An ant can lift fifty times its own weight—with its mouth.

- The common snail has close to ten thousand teeth—all on its tongue.

- A frog must close its eyes in order to swallow.

- Texas horned toads can squirt blood from the corners of their eyes.

- The tumbler pigeon can do backward somersaults while flying.

- The praying mantis is the only insect that can turn its head without moving any other part of its body.

- If it were possible to weigh all of the land animals on the surface of the Earth, ants would be 10 to 15 percent of the total weight.

- Scientists have determined that the common housefly hums in the musical key of F.

- To make 1 pound (454 g) of honey, bees must collect nectar from approximately two million flowers.

- Most mammals live for about 1.5 billion heartbeats.

- A mosquito has forty-seven teeth.

ECOSYSTEMS NEAR AND FAR

An ecological system—*ecosystem* for short—is made up of organisms that live together. All living things that come together in one place make up a community or ecosystem. Plant or animal, community members depend on one another for survival. Some animals eat plants, some plants live off other plants, and some animals eat other animals. All living things are part of one or more food chains—energy and materials are passed along the line from one living thing to another in the form of food.

Just as all other living things depend on one another, humans, too, need a variety of plants and animals in order to survive. Understanding how all living things rely on each other is an important part of nature study. The experiments in this chapter will allow you to journey into the ecosystems that exist where you are.

Life in a Square

You may be surprised to discover a wide variety of life—right in your own backyard.

You need:

4 sharpened pencils or sticks

piece of string about 4$\frac{1}{2}$ feet (135 cm) long

a hand lens or magnifying glass

a notebook or journal

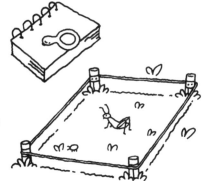

WHAT TO DO:

Go into your yard or a nearby park. Push the pencils into the soil to form a 1-foot (30 cm) square. Tie string around them, making a miniature "boxing ring" on the ground. Get down and look closely inside the square. Make a note of all the different types of plants you see there, as well as the varieties of animal life and their behavior as they travel (jump, crawl, slither) through it. Go back regularly over several weeks to observe and record what you see.

WHAT HAPPENS:

You have a long list of natural life that lives in or has passed through your marked-off square. In fact, you are probably amazed at the many different forms of life that you found in just that very small space!

WHY:

Life is everywhere! Take the time to stop, see what is going on around you, and wonder at all the life forms that share the environment you call home. You may discover animals and plants, living in your own backyard, that you never knew existed!

Happy Habitat

How would you like to be the creator of your own miniature ecosystem?

You need:
a 2- or 3-liter plastic soda bottle
pebbles
aquarium charcoal
soil
water
small plants (see below)
small animals (see below)
string or rubber band
piece of lightweight cloth

WHAT TO DO:

Have an adult cut off the top of the plastic soda bottle. Cover the bottom of the bottle with a layer of small pebbles mixed with bits of aquarium charcoal. Put in a layer of soil about twice as deep as the first layer. Sprinkle the soil with just enough water to keep it moist (you may have to add water occasionally).

Place several plants, such as mosses, ferns, lichens, or liverworts (available from the garden or aquarium shop), into the soil. You could sprinkle a few grass seeds on the soil, too. Place several rocks or pieces of wood into the bottom of the bottle.

Some small land animals (such as snails, earthworms, a tiny turtle, or a frog) can also be added. To allow humidity and ventilation place some lightweight cloth over the top holding it on with a rubber band or tying it there with a string. Another option is to substitute the cloth with the bottom of another plastic soda bottle of the same size. Cut 4 inches (10 cm) off the bottom and usepush pins to create ventilation holes in the cover. Keep the bottle out of direct sunlight and be sure to feed the occupants of your habitat regularly.

WHAT HAPPENS:

Your miniature ecosystem will grow and flourish as long as you add some moisture occasionally. If you put animals in the bottle, check with your local pet store for an appropriate food supply.

WHY:

This ecosystem is similar to a wetlands or woodlands ecosystem in nature. Plants and animals are able to survive because they are dependent on each other and because all of their needs (air, water, food) are provided in their immediate environment.

A Simple Community

Here's how you can construct a simple and inexpensive aquarium in your own home.

You need:

a commercial-size mayonnaise jar
  (from your school cafeteria or a local restaurant)
gravel
sand
aquatic plants (see below)
guppies or goldfish
water snails
wire screen
fish food

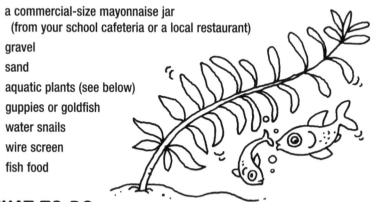

WHAT TO DO:

Wash and rinse out the large jar thoroughly. Wash and rinse the gravel and sand, too. (Clean gravel and sand can be obtained at an aquarium store.) Place a $1/2$-inch (1 cm) layer of gravel on the bottom of the jar; add a 1-inch (2.5 cm) layer of sand on top of the gravel. Fill the jar almost to the top with tap water and allow the jar to sit undisturbed for three to four days so that the chlorine in the water can evaporate. Get two or three aquatic plants (such as elodea) from an aquarium store and place them in the bottom of the jar (make sure they are firmly rooted in the sand). Place two or three goldfish and a few snails in the jar. Place a piece of wire screening over the top of the jar to keep in the snails.

WHAT HAPPENS:

This miniature environment will be able to sustain itself for some time (so long as you put in some fish food occasionally).

The plants and animals will thrive for a good while, but you may need to obtain an inexpensive air pump later to keep your aquarium going.

WHY:

Plants and animals need each other in order to survive. In an aquatic environment, such as your aquarium, the plants provide necessary oxygen for the fish and snails. The fish provide nourishment (with their wastes) for the plants (and the eventual growth of small plants such as algae). The algae serve as a food source for the snails.

When properly maintained, this miniature ecosystem will be in balance.

Houses and Homes

Where do animals live? What kind of dwelling places do they call home? Let's take a look around.

You need:
a notebook
a camera with film

WHAT TO DO:
With an older friend or adult, take a walking field trip around your town or neighborhood. Look for places where animals live—nests, burrows, tree trunks, anthills, under rocks, in and near logs, holes in the ground, even cracks in the sidewalk. If you have a camera, take a photograph of each **habitat**, or place where an animal lives, or draw a picture of it. Later, name the animals and match their pictures with the pictures of their "houses." An older brother or sister, parent, or high school student might enjoy helping you learn the scientific names of the animals to add to your journal or field trip report.

WHAT HAPPENS:

You will be amazed to discover the wide variety of animals living in homes in and near your own house. You will probably discover that you've found many more than you thought you would.

WHY:

Animals are everywhere, from high in the trees to far under the ground. The homes that animals live in are designed to protect their young, shelter the animals from the weather, and help them defend against their enemies, and they are located where they can find the food they need. In fact, aren't those the same reasons why humans live where they do?

My Own Backyard

Did you know that your backyard can qualify as a nature preserve—a place where plants and animals are protected?

The National Wildlife Federation sponsors the Backyard Wildlife Habitat program. Their Web site, at www.nwf.org/ backyardwildlifehabitat/, will provide you with information and details about establishing your backyard as a wildlife preserve. For a small fee, you can even have your yard certified as an official Backyard Wildlife Habitat.

Bags of Bananas

Decomposition, the natural decay of dead organisms, is a continuing process in nature. You can learn about it by doing this experiment in your own home.

You need:

4 sealable plastic sandwich bags
a banana
a knife
2 packets yeast
water

WHAT TO DO:

Label the four bags A, B, C, and D. In bag A put several slices of banana; in bag B put several slices of banana and the contents of a packet of yeast; in bag C put several slices of banana and some water; and in bag D put several slices of banana, some water, and the contents of a packet of yeast. Seal all the bags and place them on a sunny windowsill for a few days.

WHAT HAPPENS:

The banana slices in bag A darken slightly. The yeast in bag B grows very slowly, but there is some change in the banana slices. The slices in bag C show some decay and some mold. The banana slices in bag D show the most decay. In that bag, the banana is breaking down. The liquid is bubbling, and carbon dioxide gas is forming and expanding the bag. The bag may pop open and release a powerful odor into the room.

WHY:

When plant and animal life die, they serve as a valuable food source for **microorganisms**. These microorganisms feed on the dead materials and break them down. Yeast is made up of millions of such microorganisms that grow under the right conditions—when moisture, food, and warmth are present. As they grow, the microorganisms in bag D break down the banana slices.

The same process takes place in nature. Microorganisms can reduce large animals and plants into valuable nutrients for the soil. In other words, when an organism dies it provides what other organisms need in order to live.

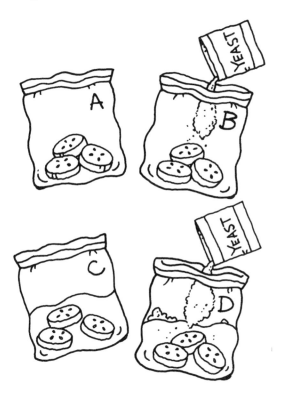

It's Absolutely Degrading

Do you know what the word *biodegradable* means? Here's how you can find out about this continuing process and how it works.

You need:

a slice of fruit (apple, orange, peach)
a slice of bread
a piece of lettuce
a plastic or Styrofoam cup
a piece of aluminum foil
a shovel
water
ice-cream sticks
pencil or felt marker

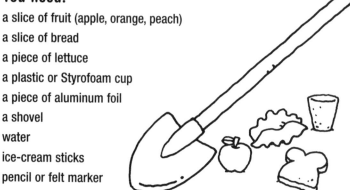

WHAT TO DO:

Find a place in your or a friend's yard where you can dig some small holes for this experiment. Dig five holes, each about 8 to 12 inches (20–30 cm) deep. Place the fruit slice in one hole, the bread in another hole, the lettuce in another, the cup in the fourth hole, and the foil in the last hole. Cover each hole with soil and water each one thoroughly. Place a marker stick saying "fruit," "bread," "lettuce," "cup," or "foil" (or anything else you are testing for biodegradability) at the location of each hole. After four to five weeks, return to the filled holes and dig up what you buried.

WHAT HAPPENS:

The fruit, bread, and lettuce have probably disintegrated (in fact, you may find it difficult even to locate these items). The rate at which these items have biodegraded depends on the amount of moisture in the soil and the soil's temperature. The cup and the piece of foil, however, will be whole and easy to locate.

WHY:

When organic matter (fruit, bread, lettuce, even dead plants and animals) is left on or in the soil, it starts to break down. This natural (and constant) biodegrading process, caused by microorganisms, releases nutrients into the soil so that other organisms can grow. The cup and the foil are not biodegradable, the microorganisms can't affect them, so they will never decompose. Landfills are filled with lots of nonbiodegradable materials that take up valuable space without returning anything to the environment.

DID YOU KNOW?

- Americans consume about 55 million tons (50 million metric tons) of food from the oceans each year, and dump 90 percent of their garbage into landfills.

- Homeowners in the United States use ten times more toxic chemicals per acre on their gardens and lawns than do farmers on the acreage where they grow food.

- Each year, more than 27 million acres (10.8 million hectares) of tropical rain forest are destroyed—an area about the size of the state of Ohio, or of Iceland.

- Although rain forests cover only about 6 percent of the Earth's surface, they contain more than half of all the plant and animal species.

- The rain forests of the Amazon Basin produce about 40 percent of the world's oxygen.

NATURE PROBLEMS TO SOLVE

How we care for the Earth and its inhabitants today will have a big impact on the word we live in twenty or fifty years from now. It will determine the kinds of food, recreation, and quality of life available to us in the years to come. Becoming a conservator (a caretaker) of the Earth is important for every man, woman, and child.

We are faced today with many problems that affect the way we live and the ways in which our plants and our animal friends live, too. Air and water pollution, toxins and trash, and the destruction of the ozone layer (which filters out the harmful rays of the sun) may someday threaten all our lives. These problems are not simple ones, and they require more than simple solutions. But if we care about our environment, and understand how we and the animals and plants must all exist side by side in order to survive, then we need to start now to work together to preserve nature.

Preserving nature won't be easy. It will take lots of planning and people working together to ensure a natural and healthy life for ourselves and for our biological neighbors. The experiments in this chapter will alert you to some of the problems we face, and suggest what you and your friends can do to help preserve our fragile environment.

A Plethora of Pollution

Pollution can take many forms. Some of it can be seen, but many types that we don't see are just as dangerous.

You need:

4 small jars, without lids
tape
felt-tip marker
water
pond soil
pond water with scum (algae)
liquid plant fertilizer
liquid detergent
motor oil (use vegetable oil as substitute)
vinegar

WHAT TO DO:

Leave the water out in a container for three to four days to let the chlorine dissipate. When the water has "aged," label the four jars A, B, C, and D. Prepare each jar as follows: fill the jar halfway with the aged water, put in a $1/2$-inch (1 cm) layer of pond soil, add 1 teaspoon (5 mL) of liquid plant fertilizer, then fill the jar the rest of the way with pond water. Allow the jars to sit in a sunny location or windowsill for two weeks.

Next, treat each separate jar as follows: to jar A add 2 tablespoons (30 mL) liquid detergent; to jar B add enough drops of motor oil or vegetable oil to cover the surface; to jar C add $1/2$ cup (120 mL) vinegar; leave jar D just as it is. Allow the jars to sit for four weeks more.

WHAT HAPPENS:

With the addition of the detergent, motor oil, and vinegar to the first three jars, the healthy growth that took place in the jars during the first two weeks of the experiment has severely changed. In fact, those jars now probably show little or no growth taking place, while the organisms in jar D continue to grow.

WHY:

Detergent, motor oil, and vinegar are pollutants that prevent organisms from obtaining the nutrients and oxygen they need to continue growing. The detergent shows what happens when large quantities of soap are released in an area's water; the motor oil shows what happens to organisms after an oil spill; and the vinegar shows what can happen when high levels of acids are added to an ecosystem such as a pond or stream. When industry, factories, homeowners, and other consumers put these and other kinds of pollutants into streams, rivers, and other sources of water, it can seriously affect and even destroy the plants and animals that live there.

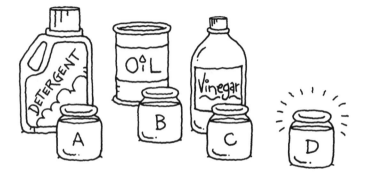

Eggs over Easy

Pollution is a problem all over the world. Let's take a look at one specific pollution problem: oil.

You need:

motor oil or vegetable oil (olive) as substitute

4 sealable plastic bags

watch or timer

masking tape

4 hard-boiled eggs

food coloring

water

felt marker

WHAT TO DO:

Label the four bags A, B, C, and D.

Fill each bag with $1/_2$ cup (120 mL) water and $1/_2$ cup (120 mL) motor oil (or vegetable oil with a few drops of food coloring). Place a hard-boiled egg in each bag. Remove the egg from bag A after fifteen minutes; remove the egg from bag B after half an hour; remove the egg from bag C after an hour; and remove the egg from bag D after two hours. Each time you remove an egg from a bag, carefully peel off the eggshell.

WHAT HAPPENS:

The eggs that remain in the oil-polluted water the longest show the most contamination. The egg in bag D, for example, has more oil inside its shell than the egg in bag A.

WHY:

When an oil tanker accident spills oil into the water, the oil slick that forms sticks to the bodies and surfaces of birds, plants, fish, and other aquatic creatures and prevents them from doing what they do naturally. (Birds cannot use their wings or fly, fish cannot breathe, and plants cannot grow.) Many living things die as a result of oil spills.

Not in *My* Air!

Do you know if there is air pollution in your area, and how much? Here's a way to find out.

You need:
petroleum jelly
3 index cards
masking tape

WHAT TO DO:

Smear a thin layer of petroleum jelly on one side of each of the three index cards. Tape two of the cards in different locations outside. For example, one card can be taped to the side of your house and the other hung from a tree branch in your backyard. Or one card can be taped to a mailbox and the other to a garage door. The third card should be taped someplace inside your home. Check the cards every week or so to see how much **particulate matter** (dust, odd bits and pieces of material, pollen, and other small particles that float in the air) have collected on them.

WHAT HAPPENS:

After some time (depending on where you live) you will find that the two cards placed outside have collected a good amount of particulate matter (the one placed inside the house may have considerably fewer particles on it). The amount of matter collected on the two outside cards indicates the amount of pollution that is in your air, and that you are probably taking into your lungs as well. (Do this air test several times throughout the seasons, to see if pollution is better, or worse, at some times than at other times.)

WHY:

Air pollution is a serious concern in many industrial areas. Factories, trucks and cars, and incinerators are just a few of the causes of air pollution. The polluting particles, often very small, can affect the environment nearby and far away (blown great distances by the wind). The pollutants settle on the ground and on buildings, and sometime we inhale them into our lungs. Your cards will show you how serious the air pollution is where you live. Your card may also include natural pollutants such as pollen or dried leaves.

Oil Change

Repeat the "Eggs over Easy" experiment, but this time also put $1/_2$ cup (120 mL) of liquid dishwashing detergent into each bag. Shake each bag gently and allow it to stand for the designated time. Notice what effect the liquid soap has on the contamination of each egg.

For another variation, put the detergent into each bag just before you remove the eggs. While the soap might remove some of the oil from the outside of the eggs, does it have any effect on the inside of the eggs?

A Band of Bands

Here's another experiment that demonstrates how much air pollution is in your area.

You need:

8 rubber bands (same size and shape)

2 wire coat hangers

a very large sealable plastic freezer bag

a magnifying lens

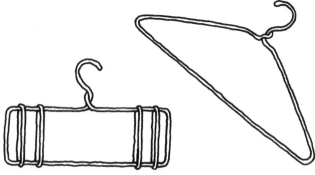

WHAT TO DO:

Bend each coat hanger into a rectangular shape. Slide two rubber bands onto one end of a coat hanger and two over the other end. The rubber bands should be fairly tight to be sure to stay on. Do this for both hangers. Hang one of the coat hangers outside (in a tree, for example), making sure it is out of the sun. Place the second hanger in a plastic bag and seal it. Keep it in your room.

Look at both hangers once a week. Use the magnifying glass to examine the condition of he rubber bands on the two hangers. Note the differences between the two sets of rubber bands.

WHAT HAPPENS:

Depending on the amount of air pollution in your local area, the rubber bands on the hanger hung outside start to deteriorate. They begin to decompose, split, or break apart.

WHY:

Pollution in the air can affect all kinds of things, even those made of rubber, so the condition of the rubber bands on the hanger placed outside is a good indication of the severity of this problem in your area. If the rubber bands break down in only a few weeks, then it probably means that there is a great deal of air pollution in your area. If, however, the rubber bands take longer to break down, there may not be as much pollution. You'll also notice that the rubber bands on the coat hanger that you kept inside the plastic bag showed no breakdown at all. This shows what can happen when air pollution is reduced or eliminated.

Acid From the Skies

Acid rain is a danger to plant life in many parts of the world. Here's why.

You need:

3 jars with lids
marking pen
water
tablespoon

masking tape
$^3/_4$ cup (180 mL) lemon juice
3 growing bean plants

WHAT TO DO:

Label the three bean plant jars A, B, and C. Put $^1/_4$ cup (60 mL) of lemon juice in each, then add water as follows: to jar A, add $^1/_4$ cup (60 mL) water; to jar B, add $^1/_2$ cup (120 mL) of water; to jar C, add $^3/_4$ cup (180 mL) of water. Place the jars on a sunny windowsill. Every day, water each plant with four tablespoons of the lemon juice solution assigned to it.

WHAT HAPPENS:

Plant A shows the effects of the "acid rain" first. The leaves start to curl and shrivel. Its growth slows down or stops. The other two bean plants eventually show these problems, too.

WHY:

Acid rain is caused by air pollutants pumped into the atmosphere through industrial smokestacks. The pollutants fall back to earth when it rains. The pollutants, which are acidic like the lemon juice, build up in the soil and affect the growth of plant life (like the lemon juice solutions did to your plants). The more acidic the rain (like solution A), the sooner the plant is affected. Over time, the plants will die, and new plants won't be able to grow because of the highly acidic soil.

That Cookie is Mine

When resources such as coal are taken from the ground, does it affect the local environment?

You need:
2 chocolate chip cookies
toothpicks
a clock or stopwatch

WHAT TO DO:

Put one cookie in the freezer for an hour, and the other in a sunny window. Then, pretending you are a coal miner, take a toothpick and "mine" as much hard "coal" (chocolate chips) from the cold cookie as you can for four minutes. Then stop, and try for four minutes more to dig the soft chips out of the cookie left in the window. How many chips can you remove from each in four minutes?

WHAT HAPPENS:

You find it hard to "mine" the chips and, in both cases, probably had to destroy or alter the "landscape" of the cookie in order to get chips out. You also notice that it is easier to "mine" hard chips than to remove soft ones.

WHY:

The hard and soft chips in the cookies represent two basic types of coal: **anthracite** (hard) coal and **bituminous** (soft) coal. When coal is mined, it can damage the surrounding area. Over several years, a good deal of harm can be done to the environment. It is often difficult or impossible to reverse the damage done by mining, just as it would be difficult to repair your cookies after removing the chocolate chips.

Gumming Up the Works

Oil spills are dangerous to the environment, so we are always looking for ways to prevent them, and to contain them when they do happen. How? Try using bubble gum to contain your own home-grown oil spill!

You need:

chunk-style bubble gum
a pie plate or shallow pan
water
household machine oil (such as 3-in-One)
toothpick
handheld grater
paper

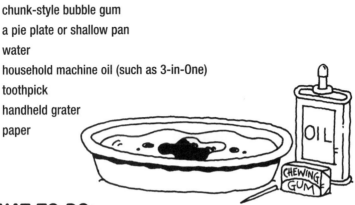

WHAT TO DO:

Put a piece of chunk-style bubble gum in the freezer and leave it overnight. Fill the pie plate halfway with water. Carefully release about 10 drops of oil into the middle of the water, then use a toothpick to pull the oil drops together. Take the bubble gum from the freezer and ask an adult to grate it into small strips onto a sheet of paper. Carefully lift the sheet and sprinkle the grated gum onto the oil spill. Let a little of it fall into the water as well. Wait for about thirty minutes.

WHAT HAPPENS:

The gum begins to absorb the oil in the water. Depending on the amount of gum you sprinkled into the oil, all or most of the spill will be absorbed. The gum strips that fell on the water don't absorb anything.

WHY:

Gum consists of a type of particle known as a **nonpolar mole-cule**. A nonpolar molecule will absorb another type of nonpo-lar molecule. Water, however, is made of polar molecules. Thus, the gum (which is nonpolar) will not absorb the water (which is polar), but will absorb the oil (which is also nonpo-lar). So, in order to contain or absorb oil spills in the ocean, it is necessary to put a nonpolar absorbing material on the spill. In this way the oil is absorbed by the material but the sea water is not. The material and the oil spill can then be skimmed or pumped from the surface of the water.

DID YOU KNOW?

- The average American family produces about 100 pounds (45 kg) of trash and garbage every week.

- According to some scientists, more than 99 percent of all the plant and animal species that have ever lived are now extinct.

- In California alone, more than 200 million tons (181 million metric tons) of pesticides are used each year.

- In the Imperial Valley in California, there is a power plant that burns about 900 tons (816 metric tons) of cow manure daily.

- Every year, landfills in the United States are crammed with 24 million tons (22 million metric tons) of leaves and grass clippings that could have been composted and recycled for use in gardens.

- By recycling a ton of paper, we can save close to 10 cubic feet (0.28 cu m) of landfill space—and seventeen trees!

- Every year humans add 6 billion tons (5.4 billion metric tons) of carbon dioxide to the atmosphere.

Most of this comes from burning fossil fuels, such as coal and oil.

Making a Difference

Kids can and do make a difference! When you and your friends, classmates, or neighbors take an interest in preserving nature, we can all work together to care for the plants, animals, and environments that are part of our world. Sometimes it may mean putting up a bird feeder in your backyard, picking up litter along the side of a road, or writing to groups and organizations for information and brochures on what you can do to help. All our efforts are important, because if we don't take care of nature, who will?

A group called **Renew America** collects stories about people and groups who are working to preserve the environment. You may be interested in learning about some of the nature activities that kids all across the country are participating in—true stories about kids who are making a difference. If so, write to them and ask for information:

Renew America
1200 18th Street, NW
Suite 1100
Washington, DC 20036
(202) 721-1545
E-mail: renewamerica@counterpart.org

INDEX